THE UTE INDIANS OF SOUTHWESTERN COLORADO

Helen Sloan Daniels

Edited by Jan & P. David Smith

WESTERN REFLECTIONS PUBLISHING COMPANY®

Lake City, CO

ISBN 978-1-932738-60-5
Library of Congress Control Number: 2008926973

Cover and book design: Laurie Goralka Design
Cover photo: 1905 Postcard, P. David Smith Collection

First Edition
Printed in the United States of America

Western Reflections Publishing Company®
P.O. Box 1149, 951 N. Highway 149
Lake City, CO 81235
1-800-993-4490
westref@montrose.net
www.westernreflectionspub.com

PROLOGUE

Helen Sloan Daniels was the third generation of her family to live in Durango, Colorado. Her grandfather, Robert Sloan, a Civil War veteran, came to Durango with the D&RG Railroad in 1881 (the year the town was established). He built a flour mill, opened a store, and in 1912 constructed a beautiful home on 3rd Avenue. Helen was born December 21, 1899 in Durango. She spent all of her life in Durango except for the time she attended the University of Colorado, where she received her degree in English literature.

Helen was a well-trained amateur anthropologist and archeologist. She was an officer in the San Juan Basin Archeological Society and served for over thirty years as a trustee of the Durango Public Library, which her grandfather helped to establish in 1906. Helen was an inveterate collector of all types of historical information, photographs, and objects; and she was very interested in Native American culture in the Four Corners area – in particular the Anasazi (now called Pueblo Ancestors), Ute, Navajo, Apache, and Hopi.

Helen Sloan Daniels was a very special person. One reporter wrote, "when she walks into a room, dignity and wisdom surround all." She became interested in archeology through helping with early "digs" with the Smithsonian Institute at Mesa Verde Park. Later she noticed city crews unearthing, and sometimes destroying, ancient artifacts at the city gravel pit. She organized a National Youth Administration group to dig, catalog, and repair items from the site (later determined to be from 300 B. C.) She also helped to excavate the Fall Creek Basketmaker site above the Animas Valley. Most of the artifacts from that site were given or loaned to Mesa Verde National Park and were displayed there for years.

Later, she drew many sketches of Ute, Anasazi, and Navajo pottery. A portion of the Durango Library is named for her and her donated collection of artifacts, pottery, drawings, and historical information about Native Americans. Helen became such an authority that *The Christian Science Monitor* in 1960 wrote, "She has made understanding and preservation of ancient Southwest culture her chief goal for some years. Her books and monographs are used as texts whenever this culture is studied and are so valued by the Library of Congress that they are kept bound in tooled leather."

In 1975 she was given the University of Colorado's Distinguished Service Award for her work as an amateur archeologist and anthropologist. She was also given the Distinguished Service Award by Ft. Lewis College in 1978. Helen was a member of the Sarah Platt Decker chapter of the DAR and spearhead an effort to record the history of her area by interviewing (or causing to be interviewed) hundreds of "old-timers" before they died. Their antidotes are now collected in one book, which is a prime resource for white history in the San Juans. Besides editing this book, Mrs. Daniels also co-authored the book *Echoes From Navajo Land* and wrote about the Basketmaker II site at Fall Creek above the Animas Valley. Helen gave many of her "treasures" to the Durango Public Library. Upon her death on May 16, 1979, she also donated much of her archeological and American Indian collection to the Center for Southwest Studies at Ft. Lewis College. There is also a Ft. Lewis scholarship given in her honor.

This book was originally mimeographed for the Durango Public Library and is copyrighted in its name. A portion of the sale of each book will go to them. It was originally published in four-color mimeograph (no small feat in itself) which was produced with young women working for the National Youth Administration, a part of the WPA. Helen and her friends drew many of the artifacts by hand directly onto the mimeograph paper (another feat, especially since there was an artist who was supposed to do the job but had used up her allotted time on the project when just halfway through). Unfortunately, despite Helen's monumental effort, Western Reflections had to redo the text (many thanks to Jan Smith) and leave out some of the drawings because they would not reproduce well. We also felt that some copyediting was necessary for the book. In fact, some of the mimeographed words are impossible to read, and we had to just make our best guess.

In reading this book it must be remembered that Helen lived and wrote almost sixty-five years ago. The attitude of many whites towards the Utes was much different than it is today, and some comments made about the Utes sound very harsh, offensive, or even cruel today. Yet, that was the white attitude at the time in Durango and throughout the West. There had been a strong effort in the Durango area to get the Utes to take their land "in severalty" or individual ownership of portions of the land rather than common ownership of the whole reservation. Taking the land in severalty would not have allocated the whole reservation and would have left tracts for whites to file on – land which the whites of the day felt would be otherwise wasted because it was not in agricultural use. The Utes themselves were split over this situation. Eventually, the Southern Utes at Ignacio took about half the reservation in severalty, and the Ute Mountain Utes kept their land in common. Today it does not seem as important to turn the Utes into farmers and ranchers as most U.S. citizens live in an urban environment. But in the 1930s and early 1940s most American citizens still lived "on the farm," and the general feeling was that every square foot of land that could be farmed or grazed should be so used.

This manuscript also shows the important role that politics had in "the Ute question." We offer this book not as proof of the facts stated herein, but as background for what happened to the Utes. It is also interesting to note the difference in white opinion – from the "bleeding heart liberals of the East" and the hard core "they are savages" attitude in the West. Many Westerners sincerely believed that Easterners just didn't understand the problem because they didn't live with Native Americans. Much of the Easterners' attitudes were formed from reading the 1881 book, *A Century of Dishonor*, by Helen Hunt, which was the true story of the mistreatment, lies, and even massacres by the United States government of Native Americans. Hunt's book did as much for Native Americans as *Uncle Tom's Cabin* did for blacks. Neither view was totally accurate or correct, but it is obvious that many Westerners had a negative and paternalistic attitude towards Native Americans.

Both Western Reflections Publishing Co. and the Durango Public Library decided that it is important to reproduce the book just as it was, without leaving out what now seems to be very negative comments. We feel that it is important to recognize the attitudes and arguments of whites from the past toward Native Americans. Some of these people were with the Utes as far back as the 1860s, and they were friendly and well-acquainted with them. However it is also obvious that many of the people were very patronizing, benevolent, or thought of the Utes as savages. Much of what is recorded in this book is not Helen's writing and should not be automatically taken as being her attitude. We include these views, unedited, so that the attitudes of the times (the 1880s and 1890s as well as the 1930s and 1940s) can be seen.

One thing is for sure. Helen Sloan Daniels cared for the Native Americans of her time, and especially the Ute Indians. One person aptly described her life as "lived with exuberance and energy, a life accustomed to taking what is offered and multiplying it to exceed by far what most would make of it." One example of that kind of life was that she felt it extremely important to preserve the Ute culture that she saw dissolving before her very eyes. This little book was painstakingly put together as a result. There are items of interest in this book that have never been mentioned since and would be totally forgotten forever if it were not for her work.

THE UTE INDIANS OF SOUTHWESTERN COLORADO

Compiled by Helen Sloan Daniels
Sketches by Pearl Oliver
Maps by Irene Waddell
Typing by Mary Nestora Sena

DURANGO PUBLIC LIBRARY MUSEUM PROJECT
NATIONAL YOUTH ADMINISTRATION
DURANGO, COLORADO
1941

TO
SADIE K. SULLIVAN
AND HER STAFF OF THE
DURANGO PUBLIC LIBRARY

ACKNOWLEDGMENT

Our gratitude is expressed to the many wise men and women who sat by our council fires and helped us to choose the thoughts to be expressed in these pages.

Miss Neil B. McCartey's *Indians of the San Juan Basin* is posthumous, by the cooperation of her sister, Mrs. George Robertson. Miss Nellie McCloud also gives consent to the use made herein of her father's report, in *The Southern Ute Indians of Colorado*. D. H. Wattson furnished the paper on *Consolidated Utes* and also the Principal Ute Legends collected by Ford C. Frick. *An Outline of Ute Indian Culture* was written by Albert M. McCall.

The Ute Medicine Man's Kit was loaned to the Durango Public Library by E. E. McKean, Jr. and was reported in *The Durango Public Library Museum Report, 1940*. At that time it was impossible to include many fine specimens of Ute craft, and the color prints in *The Ute Medicine Man's Kit* inspired us to continue this report with as many more color prints as we could achieve with mimeograph methods. (Two stencils were cut in 1937 by James G. Allen repeated here in the three color print "Sun Dance Bone Whistles" and "Sun Dance Rattles" used in *"Sundancing by Moonlight."*)

We are deeply grateful for the loan of the artifacts to be included in this report from the following persons:

To Mrs. J.J. Musser for the loan of the Cradle Board; Neckband; Feather Headdress; Pipe; Cone Water Jug; Drum; and Sun Dance Fan.

To Mr. E. E. McKean, Jr., our thanks for the loan of the Wedding Basket and the Sioux Gourd Rattle, as well as the Ute Medicine Man's Kit.

To Miss Sadie K. Sullivan, our thanks for the loan of the doll and several sets of bows and arrows.

To Senator George E. West, our thanks for the gift of the saddle blanket.

Mr. Walter E. Weightman was interested in collecting Ute materials and some of his collection is now in the Denver Art Museum and also at the Laboratory of Anthropology at Santa Fe. The Bone Breastplate*; War Club, Braid Ornaments*; Flute; Pipe Bag*; Awl Case*; and Vanity Case* were loaned by Dr. and Mrs. Daniels and the asterisk marks those which came from the Weightman Collection.

Cover designs for sections are mainly suggested by studies of photographs and an extensive file of clippings, and are used in exemplifying the text. A collection of photographs from the Gonner Studio, Pennington Studio, and Fishback Studio in Durango, the Millarky Studio at Gallup, the Walker Studio at Montrose, with postcards sold at the Fort Hall Trading Post on the Shoshonean Reservation, Idaho, helped us to justify our pleasure when a little girl who was watching our sketching squealed delightedly, "It's real!"

It has been our intention to keep it real. Help in attaining that mark has been generously accorded by Albert Ellington, mimeograph company representative, with his patient coaching in the technique of combining color plates.

These have all been our helpers, but our mainstay has been Miss Sadie K. Sullivan, and our thanks must here be recorded for many hours of coaching which she has put in with our clerical assistants provided by the National Youth Administration.

Helen Sloan Daniels

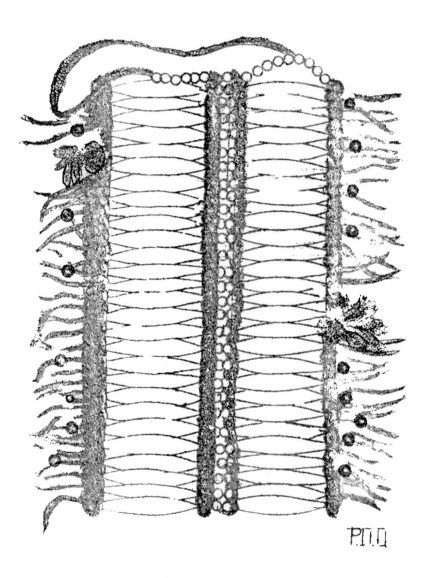

BONE BREASTPLATE

Early photographs indicate a prevalence of these boned breastplates among the Sioux and northern mountain tribes. A few are now seen on exhibition; only one was shown at Gallup, New Mexico, at the Inter Tribal Ceremonial of 1940, a collector's item that was not for sale. Another breastplate was shown at a display in Phoenix, Arizona, and the origin of the bone was acclaimed "Deer shin-bone." (See "Deer of the World" National Geographic Magazine, *October 1939, page 473. According to a detailed study of deer leg anatomy, the small bone below the knee varies according to the specie, a very hard ivory-like bone, four inches long in the mule deer species.)*

Although of Indian design, it came into general use after the whites settled the country, for metal bits are necessary to drill the centers, so that the bone may be strung on thongs. A valuable transition example, a blend of skills, the steel tool is necessary, but it is applied to Indian ornament.

This information was supplied by Miss Frances Reynolds at the Denver Art Museum.

Photographs show some variety in the methods of tying and adding additional beads. The beads used in this breastplate might have been cast from bullet shells.

Women also wear these bone ornaments but the method of stringing changes. She wears long, narrow panels vertically strung, not joined at the center. The strands reach from collar to hem of dresses, sometimes of several bones forming a wide panel, and sometimes a few are joined to form a narrow panel.

Breastplate is 9 1/2 " wide, 17 1/2" long, 40 pairs of bones 4 1/2" long, 132 brass beads, neck thong 18 1/2 ".

CONTENTS

ILLUSTRATIONS

Pearl D. Oliver sketched the illustrations that are mimeographed in colors. Each illustration is sketched from an object loaned to the Durango Public Library, and we had intended to print them in several colors. In March 1941, Pearl D. Oliver was dropped from the project because she had been assigned her allotted time. When she was dropped the burden of printing then fell upon Mrs. Daniels and Julia Garcia, as well as the sketches for the section covers and for the legends. *(Editor's note —missing illustrations were not reproducible.)*

INDIANS OF THE SAN JUAN BASIN

By Nell B. McCartey

INDIANS OF THE SAN JUAN BASIN

By Nell B. McCartey

The Utes are the typical Colorado Indian. They are an important tribe of Shoshone stock. They have occupied the mountains of Colorado and the eastern part of Utah since they were first known by the white man, and they have no tradition of having come from another part of the United States. The State of Utah is named from them, "Top of the Mountain." They have usually been at peace with their neighbors and kindred in Colorado, but they have in the past incessantly warred with the Navajos.

They are subdivided in bands, of which the principle ones are the Tabeguache (Pine River), Moache, Capote, Southern Utes, Weminuche, Yampa, and Utah. Some of these will be preserved as place names in geography. Tabeguache means the people who live on the warm side of the mountain. This is the band to which our Southern Utes belong. Tabeguache is a beautiful and fitting name for the Indians who have made their home in the beautiful Pine River Valley where the high mountains on all sides shield them from cold winds and where the sun shines most of the year.

In 1776, when our forefathers were declaring their independence from England and making the beginning of our own United States, Escalante, a Spanish explorer, starting from Santa Fe, one of the oldest cities in the Spanish possessions in America, and explored all through the San Juan Basin. He was charmed with the beauty and fertility of the land. He called the snowy La Platas the San Joaquins. He explored through Disappointment Country, The Paradox Valley, across the Uncompahgre Plateau, up the Gunnison and down the White River into northeastern Utah, and the Unitah Mountains. These Spanish explorers found a band of friendly Utes on the Dolores River and from there on had a Ute guide. At that time, the lodge pole trails were to be seen all through this country.

Some of the Utes came into frequent contact with the Spaniards at the trading post. Some few Jesuit priests came to them. In this way some Spanish words filtered into the Ute language and have been added to by latter association and intermarriage with the Mexicans. We could hardly say that the Utes gained any appreciable Spanish culture. Before the Spaniards came, the Utes had no horses. By the introduction of horses the Spanish had a great influence on the mode of living. Two centuries ago the Spanish cavaliers brought cargoes of horses with them to America. The Utes were near the New Mexico border and soon learned the pleasure of the companionship of horses and the advantages of hunting on horseback. They were one of the first tribes to use horses.

All the territory west of the foothills belonged to the Utes. The Utes formally recognized the U.S. Government in 1849. This, as you will notice, was shortly after the Mexican War and the cession of New Mexico to the U. S. Again in 1863 they made a treaty at Conejos to keep within their natural boundaries in Colorado and New Mexico. In 1868 the Senate ratified a treaty whereby two agencies were to be established for the Utes. One was for Unitah and Yampah bands on the White River in new Rio Blanco County. The other was for the Southern Utes on Pine River. Wild horses drifted through the Rockies in great droves and could have been secured by the Utes coming from the Spanish settlements. Taos agency was the first.

Ouray was chief of the Tabeguache band, but it was necessary in making a treaty to have one chief for all the Utes, so Ouray was the chief. Ouray and his wife Chipeta were both exceptional Indians. It was a wise choice but did not meet with universal favor. He was given an annuity of $1,000 by the government and this made him an object of envy. The White River Utes especially resented that a chieftain should have been chosen from the Tabeguache band. In 1875 they conspired against him and accused him of misappropriating funds to pay for his sheepherders. Again in 1879 they came very near undoing his good work as peacemaker by engaging in the Meeker Massacre.

The cause of the Meeker Massacre was the removing of the Utes to this agency on White River. The Utes had been given by this treaty territory three hundred miles by two hundred miles in width in southwestern Colorado. A large part of this land was mountainous and rich in minerals. It was due to Chief Ouray that the mineral lands were ceded back to the government. The Utes resented losing Middle Park and other hunting grounds. The agents lacked tact in carrying out the instructions of the government. The Indians were sullen and ugly. The agent was fearful of results and the Denver papers exaggerated the difficulties. It is probable that in the old files of those papers much first-hand material could be gleaned.

Miss Meeker and some others from the Agency were captives for twenty-three days. In her account we find descriptions of the customs of the Indians fifty years ago.

The description of a war dance is typical. The Indians gathered around a pile of sage brush on which they placed a soldier's uniform. They were dressed in their best finery and decorated with feathers and fur. Two or three began the dance and others joined until they had a circle a hundred feet in circumference. Some few squaws joined the circle. The Indians would charge the pile of brush with their knives and would pretend that they were going to burn it. They became almost insane with frenzy and excitement. They kept it up for hours. It seems that even a savage race must "strafe" the enemy until through excitement enough hatred is engendered to overcome the more kindly instincts of the race. Savages do it with their war dances and civilized nations do it with the jingo journalism and war like speeches.

White people are not usually admitted to the tepees when the Utes sing their medicine songs over the sick. The medicine man kneels close to the sufferer with his back to the spectators while he sings a series of high-keyed grunts gradually reducing the pitch to a lower and more solemn tone. It is a weird sound when the family joins and the howls can be heard sometimes for a mile. They end the howl with a gurgling sound as if the throat were full of water. Then they all laugh and visit and then repeat the ceremony. Within the last year I have known of the medicine men of the Utes at Ignacio conducting a ceremony similar to this to the great disgust of the white women who have been ministering to the sick one in our more modern way.

Ouray lived over on the Uncompahgre. He had a house with carpets, stoves, curtains, and lamps. His wife, Chipeta, has recently died at a great age. (editor's note—Chipeta died almost fifty years after Ouray.) She was a high-minded Ute woman. In 1880 Ouray came to Ignacio to confer with some of the lesser chiefs and with four commissioners from Washington. While they were waiting for the gentlemen from Washington, Ouray became sick with kidney trouble and died. At that time the Indians were living in tepees. Buckskin Charley claims that he died near where the agency pumping station is now located and that he was buried two miles south of Ignacio. His burial place has been located by both Buckskin Charley and by Colorow who may be the same Colorow concerned in the Meeker Massacre. Both of these old Indians lived in La Plata County and ought to know. It is the custom of the Utes to kill two horses when a brave dies and let their carcasses lie beside the new made grave. It is probable that this custom is a burial sacrifice and that the Indian does not expect the departed brave to ride these horses in the Happy Hunting Ground. To the Indian the horse is one of his dearest possessions and is the most fitting burial sacrifice.

Since this place can be identified by Indians now living, it might be well to have it marked in a suitable manner. The hill is a rocky untillable place and any marker should conform to the landscape. This seems more practical than to remove the bones to the Indian cemetery as has been suggested.

An eye witness told me how Rabbit and his family ate. Rabbit is a well known Indian whose home is on the La Plata south of Ft. Lewis. The food is cooked altogether, the grain and the meat. It is then turned into an often used sheepskin, and each guest is supposed to reach in and get his with his hand. This is rather hard for me to believe because the children of the family attend the public school and look clean and well fed.

The children that go to the Allen Day School near Bayfield are taught to make bread and to eat as we do. They are very fond of pumpkin and squash and eat it as we do apples. They go home overnight, and it is one of the great problems of the teachers to teach them to keep clean. Their clothes are furnished by the government and the price of them is taken out of the money apportionment. The fact that there are always more in the storehouse makes it difficult to teach them to be thrifty.

The children in the country and in the villages go to the public schools. The agent insists that they attend regularly and will act as a truant officer if absences are reported to him. Pauline Buffalo, a little Indian girl who is about as broad as she is long, attends school at La Beca. She is a common type with broad face, bobbed hair, well-made stout shoes, and comfortable clothes. She lives in a square adobe house built by the government. Her parents probably own 160 acres of bottom land, and a good team of horses, and perhaps a few goats.

A few years ago a Mrs. Washington attracted my attention because she so faithfully brought her little daughter to school on horseback. They would stop a short way from the school and say a fond farewell. She was a blanketed squaw and they lived in a tepee, but she seemed to appreciate the opportunity offered her children. This year in the same school we have a bright little Indian girl as a beginner. Her name is Sunshine Cloud, a poetic name.

Occasionally an Indian finishes the eighth grade. Then they are sent away to school. Not many of them advance beyond the fourth grade. They are not very responsive pupils.

This fall a young Indian man and a girl in her teens came to see me. The girl had finished the eighth grade in a country school and had gone to Santa Fe for a year. She wanted to enter Ft. Lewis and wanted Principal Snyder or me to write directly to Washington to get the funds for her schooling. Of course this could not be done in that way. The following week the boy came back and made some more inquiries about the Fort Lewis School and then asked me how she could go to high school in Durango. I told him and he seemed much interested, asked for paper, pen and ink. He sat at the table and wrote a three page letter in good writing. A few days later Mr. McKean stopped me on the way through Ignacio and told me that she had gone to the Indian School at Riverside, California. I think that this little incident shows that the younger generation of Indians is more advanced in civilization and that they want the advantage of better ways of living.

SOURCE OF THE INDIANS OF
THE SAN JUAN BASIN

By

Helen Sloan Daniels

"Indians of the San Juan Basin" was written about the last year of Miss McCartey's life. She was at that time in her seventh term of office as Superintendent of La Plata County Schools. She was an active member of the D. A. R. Sarah Platt Decker Chapter of Durango, Colorado. This paper was written for and delivered at a program and deals with both Navajo and Ute Indians. Part II is reprinted here. Some years after Miss McCartey's death, Mrs. Hazel Robertson was secretary of the D. A. R. Chapter and loaned their copy of the paper to me so that a copy could be made.

Miss McCartey has two sisters living. One is a Durango resident, Mrs. George Robertson, who has graciously given us permission to mimeograph the story in order that it may be distributed to schools and libraries. Another sister, Mrs. I. D. Parmeter, a resident of Santa Barbara, California, has other papers of Miss McCartey's including her poems and stories in her inimitable style which we hope some day to see in print.

Phrases in Miss McCartey's story are reminiscent and the persons mentioned in it take one back through the years. A proper monument to Ouray was then in the thoughts of us all and Miss McCartey mentioned the desirability of dedicating a monument. That hope has been realized and a Chieftain Monument has been erected in Ignacio.

Samson Rabbit is still living at his home on the La Plata, south of Ft. Lewis. Ft. Lewis is now a Junior College, and the memory of Principal Snyder is still revered. Shadows of the First World War are to be seen in her phrasing of "strafe" and "jingo journalism."

One portion of Miss McCartey's story of Buckskin Charley has been transferred to a detailed description of the Chieftain's Memorial Monument now at Ignacio, Colorado. Superintendant McKean is the owner of the Ute Medicine Man's Kit which was loaned to the Durango Public Library in 1936. This unique bundle is analyzed with a detailed description and sketchs, and available in memographed form in the Durango Public Library Project Report for 1940. Some of the ornaments in the kit are worn or carried in the Sun Dance.

SOUTHERN
UTE INDIANS
OF COLORADO

By
Adair Wilson
B. W. Ritter
Richard McCloud

THE SOUTHERN UTE INDIANS OF COLORADO

By Adair Wilson, B. W. Ritter, Richard McCloud

Shall the pending agreement with them be ratified by Congress?

To the Hon. Senators and Representatives of the Congress of the United States.

In 1888 a commission appointed under a law of Congress negotiated an agreement with the Southern Ute Indians which provided among other things for the removal of these Indians from Colorado to a reservation in southeastern Utah. A bill for the ratification of this agreement is now pending in Congress. As this bill has provoked some discussion in which much lack of knowledge of the true situation and some misrepresentations have been displayed, the undersigned, a committee appointed therefore by the Board of Trade of the City of Durango, Colorado, in behalf both of the Indians and of the white citizens residing near them, beg leave to submit the following plain statement of facts.

FORMER TREATIES AND AGREEMENTS

At the close of the Mexican War the Ute Indians (Utah Indians, as then called) were settled in the portion of the territory acquired from Mexico called New Mexico. The first treaty with them was negotiated in Abiqui, N. M. December 30, 1849, by Indian Agent James S. Calhoun (U. S. Statutes at Large, Vol. 9, Pg. 984). This was simply a treaty of peace and amity, recognizing the sovereignty of the United States and stipulating that the Indians should "not depart from their accustomed homes or locations without permission. No attempt was made to define the boundaries of any reservation."

The next treaty was negotiated at Conejos, Colorado Territory, October 7, 1863, with the Tabeguache band of Ute Indians, which band did not then and does not now include any of the bands known as the Southern Ute Indians. By this treaty the boundaries of the reservation for this band were defined by natural objects and embraced lands both in Colorado and New Mexico (U. S. Statutes at Large, vol. 13, pg. 673). By this treaty the Tabeguache further agreed that the Mohuaches (a small band which is now one of the three bands known as Southern Utes) should be settled with them.

The next treaty was negotiated at Washington, D. C., March 2, 1868, with the representatives of all the Ute bands comprising the Ute tribe (U. S. Statutes at Large, vol. 15, pg. 619). By the terms of this treaty the boundaries of the reservation were again defined, and were fixed wholly in Colorado, in the western portion thereof, embracing within its limits what is now known as the Southern Ute reservation.

The next treaty (agreement then called) was entered into with all of the confederated bands at the Los Pinos agency in Colorado in 1873, and was approved April 29, 1874 (U. S. Statutes at Large, vol. 18, part 3, pg. 36). By the terms of this agreement the Utes ceded to the United States for a monetary equivalent principally, a portion of their territory as fixed by the Treaty of 1868, that portion which contained the San Juan mining region. It left to the Indians from their old territory as defined in 1868, a strip fifteen miles wide along the border line between Colorado and New Mexico, the same strip which is now occupied by the Southern Utes. A strip of twenty miles in width was also left to them along the western border of Colorado and all that part of their reservation as defined in 1868 lying north of a line ten miles north of the 38th parallel of north latitude.

Soon after this the Indian Bureau, realizing that the reservation was in very bad shape and that these fifteen and twenty mile strips were entirely unsuited for the use of the Indians, suggested that negotiations be entered into with the Southern Utes for cession of these strips. The agents of the Indians had reported that the shape of the reservation was very unsatisfactory.

In his report of 1878 their agent F. H. Weaver, said:

"Experience has shown that the shape into which this reservation has been thrown has been very unfortunate. A strip of ground fifteen miles wide with herds of cattle from both sides pouring in upon it, eating up all the grass, is no place to keep Indians."

Acting upon these suggestions an act of Congress was passed in 1878 authorizing such a negotiation. (U. S. Statutes at Large, vol. 20, p. 48).

Under this authority a commission consisting of General Hatch, Hon. Lot M. Morrill and Hon. N. C. McFarland, was appointed, and during that same year they negotiated an agreement with the Southern Utes by which they were to exchange these strips for another reservation. Before this could be acted upon by Congress, however, the outbreak of 1879 occurred.

In 1879 there was a bloody outbreak at the White River Agency of the Utes, which resulted in the massacre of Agent Meeker and his employees, the brutal captivity of the women at the agency, and the disastrous defeat of the United States troops under Captain Thornburg. A fierce Indian war was imminent but was averted by the prompt and decisive actions of the Government assisted materially by Ouray, who was recognized by the Government as the head chief of the whole tribe. A number of chiefs and head men of the various bands were taken to Washington, at which place on March 6, 1880, a new agreement was entered into with them, which was afterwards ratified by the several bands. (U. S. Statutes at Large, vol. 21, p. 199).

By the terms of this agreement the Utes ceded the whole of their reservation in Colorado to the United States, except such lands, if any, as might be allotted to them in severalty.

The Southern Utes agreed to remove to and be settled upon the unoccupied agricultural lands on the La Plata River in

Colorado, and if there should not be sufficiency of such lands on the La Plata River and its vicinity in Colorado, then upon such other unoccupied lands as may be found on the La Plata River or in its vicinity in New Mexico.

The Uncompahgres were to settle upon lands on the Gunnison and Grand Rivers, in Colorado, if a sufficiency of unoccupied lands could be found; if not, then in Utah.

The White River Utes were to be settled at Unitah, in Utah.

A commission was then appointed to secure the consent of the remaining Indians to the agreement to carry its provisions into effect.

This consent was secured, but before the agreement could be carried into effect, there became imminent danger of a serious conflict between the Indians and the Whites. The Uncompahgre and White River Utes were hurried off to the Unitah reservation, but the Southern Utes were left just where they were before the agreement was entered into, the commission reporting that there was not sufficient land for them on the La Plata River and vicinity in Colorado, and that they did not have the time to make a sufficient examination elsewhere.

This anomalous condition of affairs – the Indians having ceded the reservation and yet remaining upon it – was naturally unsatisfactory both to whites and Indians. The latter still insisted, however, that they did not wish to take lands in severalty, and so insisted at the time of making the 1880 agreement, as fully appears from the report of the commission. They urged that they be permitted to remain together and that they be removed to another reservation.

During the years intervening between 1881 and 1885 several bills were introduced in Congress looking to this end, but none became a law, nor, indeed, were actively pressed.

About the close of 1885, the agent of these Southern Utes, Mr. C. F. Stollsteimer, urgently called the attention of the Indian Office to the necessity of some action in the premises, and in consequence he was directed to bring some of the head men to Washington. The Indians came early in 1886. A bill was then pending in Congress to remove them to the identical reservation contemplated by this last agreement. They appeared before the proper committees of both Houses and expressed their approval of the measure.

DESIRE OF THE INDIANS FOR REMOVAL AND THEIR EFFORTS TO SECURE IT

The following extract from the report of the Senate Committee (Report No. 836, 49th Congress, 1st Session) shows the character of the statements and wishes of the Indians:

"In the matter of the proposed removal of the Southern Utes from Colorado to Utah

"Hearing before the Senate Committee on Indian Affairs, March 4, 1886—

"TESTIMONY OF BUCKSKIN CHARLEY
(A. D. Archuleta, interpreter)

"Question. What do you come here for? Answer. We come here to see if we cannot exchange our reservation for another.

"Q. Where do you want the new reservation located? A. We want to go west of the present reservation.

"Q. Why is it better to go that way? A. The present reservation is narrow and long and we want to go west and see if we can't sell it.

"Q. Would they want to become self-supporting? A. We want to go west and get grass land and raise stock. Where we are, we do not live comfortably. It snows so much in the winter that we are obliged to go to some place else, and we would like to have some sheep and go west. Another reason why we want to go is that the other Indians, the Navajos, are west, and we want to get near them. We live too far from them and cannot visit them without traveling very far.

"Q. If you should go to a new reservation would you like to have a boarding school built for your children? A. We are willing to send our children to school, but not away from home, because when they go away they die, and we cannot account for it.

"TESTIMONY OF CHIEF IGNACIO

"Question. What do you come here for? Answer. We came here to see the Senators and see what they can do for us. We have stated what we want and expect the Senators will do something for us.

"Q. Do you agree with Chief Charley in what he said? A. Yes; that is all right. Whatever Charley has said is straight.

"Q. Have you got any stock? A. I have got some sheep.

"Q. How many sheep? A. Very few.

"Q. How many? A. About a hundred.

"Q. What do you do with the wool? A. I sell it.

"Q. What do you do with the money, when you get it? A. I have got a mouth. I buy things to eat.

"Q. What do you do in the summer? A.I worked all summer in a ditch, but the water did not run through it.

"Q. Have you got any children? A. No; they died last summer.

"Q. Do all the Indians of your tribe want to move west? A. Yes.

"TESTIMONY OF CHIEF TA-PU-CHET

"Q. Have you talked with Charley about moving west? A. Yes, we all want to go west."

Embodied in this same report was a letter from the Commissioner of Indian Affairs, Hon. J. D. C. Atkins, of date April 5, 1886. The following extracts show the views of his Department as to the necessity of removal:

"Accordingly, I have the honor to state that it is the declared wish of the Southern Ute Indians to remove from their present reservation; but it appears they do not desire to be consolidated with or settled amongst either of the other Ute tribes. They are very much dissatisfied with their present reservation, and the first proposition looking to their removal came from the Indians themselves. This dissatisfaction is due in large measure to the disadvantages arising from the unfortunate position and configuration of their reservation, which is 110 miles in length by only fifteen miles in width. There are populous villages and towns in close proximity to the reservation both on the north and the south, and a large rural population for many miles around. The rivers which are numerous, cross the reserve from north to south and thoroughfares are, and of necessity must be kept open for travelers and commerce between these settlements. The Indians find it difficult to keep their stock from roaming beyond the narrow limits of their reserve, and they are constantly annoyed by encroachments from the outside.

"They are pastoral people, and altogether own 4,000 head of horses and mules, about the same number of sheep, besides several hundred head of cattle. Although they number 983 souls, they have but 200 acres of land under cultivation. With few exceptions, they show but little inclination to engage in agricultural pursuits.

"It would be next to impossible to close up the thoroughfares across the reservation. To do that would be to erect a 'Chinese wall' 110 miles long virtually cutting off all trade and intercourse between the large and constantly increasing communities on either side of the reservation; and yet as a matter of fact we are bound by solemn treaty stipulations with these Indians to prevent white people from entering upon or crossing said reservation.

"As it is, the Indians are in constant trouble. Difficulties are of frequent occurrence, and the relations existing between the Indians and whites are becoming more and more strained. Indeed, they have not always escaped actual conflict. Under the circumstances it is idle to expect that they will make any advancement where they are. In their present position and surroundings they are helpless. This is so apparent that they realize it themselves and ask to be removed, declaring that they are heartily tired of the constant turmoil in which they have lived ever since the whites came into their country.

"It is the decided opinion of this office that these Indians should be removed from Colorado."

That the Indians were anxious that this bill should become a law is further shown by the following extract from a report of Mr. Stollsteimer, their agent, to the Commissioner of Indian Affairs, in August, 1886:

"About the close of the year 1885 most of the chiefs and head men of the bands comprising the tribe interviewed me in reference to a removal to a more desirable reservation, giving as reasons for their desire to remove that their present reservation was not desirable on account of its formation, being a narrow strip 15 miles wide by 110 miles long. That the agency was located in the eastern part, in consequence of which (the greater part of them live to the westward) they were often compelled to go to the agency for rations and other purposes under great difficulties. That owing to the great depth of snow, the almost impassible conditions of roads caused by swollen streams and on account of the peculiar shape of the reservation, they have the greatest difficulties in keeping their herds from going off and mingling with those of the whites, and that their failure to do so has involved them in disputes with the whites.

"That they are now unable to keep their herds upon the reservation, and also unable to keep those belonging to the whites off.

"These chiefs and head men requested that their wishes for removal be laid before the Department, which request was forwarded by a communication to the Hon. Commissioner of Indian Affairs, December 28, 1885, the result of which was that authority was granted me to go to Washington with a delegation of the chiefs for the purpose of conferring with the authorities in reference to the matter.

"Their grievances were laid before the Department after which they returned to their reservation full of hope that their wishes would be gratified and at an early day be removed to a reservation meeting their wants and wishes.

"Their desire for removal from this location was increased during this summer into a constant clamor and muttering. They are daily expressing their discontent coupled with threats that they intend to leave the reservation without authority."

Before the bill came up for passage, however, a delegation of cattle-owners, who desire to retain for their occupancy as free grazing ground that portion of the proposed reservation, known as the "Blue Mountain Section," came to Washington and secured an amendment of the bill making the eastern boundary of the reservation a line forty-five miles west of the Colorado line, which was the boundary originally fixed. This took out the best part of the reservation, was very unsatisfactory to the Indians and the amendment killed the bill.

NEGOTIATION OF THE AGREEMENT NOW PENDING BEFORE CONGRESS

In 1887 Commissioner Atkins paid a personal visit to these Indians and spent several days at their agency.

During the following winter, early in the first session of the 50th Congress, a bill was introduced authorizing the appointment of a commission to treat with these Indians for their removal. It was again endorsed by Commissioner Atkins and the Interior Department, and the bill became a law.

Under its authority a commission was appointed which in 1888, negotiated the agreement, the bill for the ratification of which is now pending before Congress.

In submitting this agreement and report of the commission to the Department for transmittal to Congress, Mr. Enright, Acting Commissioner of Indian Affairs said:

"I have carefully examined the agreement and believe it to be just and favorable alike to the Government and the Indians – to the Government because if accepted and carried into effect, it will open to white settlement a very considerable area of country, hither completely locked up in free and unrestricted possession of which is absolutely necessary for the development of the vast mineral and agricultural resources of that section as is manifested from a mere glance at the map – to the Indians because they have found by experience that they cannot live in peace when they are under the conditions as now existing; that it would be next to impossible to close up the numerous thoroughfares already established across the reservation, or to prevent the opening of others, to meet the natural wants of the large and constantly increasing population on the other side of the reservation with the inevitable result of crowding them to the wall, by so circumscribing their limits as to render their chief occupation, cattle and sheep raising, utterly impossible, and by keeping them in a constant state of turmoil and conflict with the whites.

"Furthermore it is easy to foresee that the rapid settlement of the western country, and increase of population, will shortly absorb all the unoccupied space now available, leaving no escape for the Indians; hence the necessity of securing a permanent home for them while there is land enough left.

"I find that this office has long felt it to be for the best interests of these Indians that they should be removed from Colorado, and has encouraged various steps proposed looking to that end, the only difficulty being to find a suitable place for their settlement and one that would be acceptable to them. They have always shown a strong repugnance to the Uintah Valley reservation but have appeared to look with considerable favor upon the country to which it is now proposed to remove them."

The commission, which negotiated this agreement was appointed by the Secretary (now Senator) Vilos and consisted of Rev. Dr. T. S. Childs, of Washington, D. C., Hon. J. Montgomery Smith of Wisconsin and Hon. R. B. Weaver, of Arkansas. Their full, exhaustive and able report has been printed and submitted to Congress.

In the 2nd session, 50th Congress, a bill was introduced to ratify this agreement. It was favorably reported by the Senate Committee and passed the Senate, but was never acted upon in the House.

Also in the 51st Congress and in each, after a careful and through investigation, a favorable report thereon was made by the House Committee on Indian Affairs, but the bill failed to receive consideration in the House – not being reached upon the Calendar.

OBJECTIONS URGED AGAINST RATIFICATION OF THE AGREEMENT

It has been objected to this agreement that it contains no provision for the maintenance of schools among the Indians. Article 9 of this agreement provides:

"All the provisions of treaties heretofore made with the Southern Ute Indians and now in force, which are not inconsistent with the provisions of this treaty are hereby reaffirmed and declared to be in force."

Article 4 of the agreement of 1880, after providing for the establishment of suitable agencies and that the Government should aid in the support of the Indians until they should become self-supporting, further provides that —

"In the meantime the United States Government will establish and maintain schools in the settlements of the Utes and make all the necessary provision for the education of their children."

This not being abrogated by or inconsistent with the agreement of 1888 is reaffirmed by it and is in force. There is ample authority in the Government to establish schools among them wherever located, and maintain them indefinitely.

It is further objected, from a sentimental point of view, that these Indians should not be removed from a region sacred to them as containing the "graves of their sires," and as being their ancestral home around which cling the tender recollections and traditions of their past. Whatever of force there might be in this argument is wholly lost in the view of the fact that the Indians themselves are eager to make the exchange and that the home of their ancestors was in New Mexico, and of themselves also, until a very recent date.

SHALL THE INDIANS TAKE ALLOTMENTS OF LAND IN SEVERALTY

Opponents of the ratification further urge that these Indians should take and be settled upon allotments of land in severalty, and engage in agricultural pursuits. If this were practicable it would be most desirable, but it is not.

The Indians with absolute unanimity object, and they are not sufficiently advanced to maintain themselves even if they were willing.

As bearing upon this, the following extraction from reports of Special Agent Eugene E. White and W. A. McKewen, clerk in charge at Ouray Agency, are interesting.

Special Agent Eugene E. White in his report of September 20, 1886, speaking of the Ute tribe says:
"There is no Indian within my knowledge lower down in the scale of civilization that the Utes. They have acquired some of the vices of civilization, though but little of its enlightenment, and but few, if any, of its virtues. Scarcely a half a score of Uintahs and White Rivers, and not one of the Uncompahgres will send their children to school. They seem to regard every suggestion of advancement as a menace to their treaty stipulations, and every effort at civilization as an innovation upon their vested rights. The most advanced members of their tribe barely know enough of the art of industry to drive a team or plant, cultivate, and harvest a crop in the crudest possible way.

"Blankets, leggings, moccasins, gee-strings, paint and feathers constitute the fashionable or prevailing Ute costume, and the brush wickeup or cloth or skin tepee is the almost universal Ute habitation.

"There are, perhaps, less than twenty-five wooden houses in the tribe, and less than that number of Indians who are ever seen entirely in citizen's dress.

"Although not marked by any sort of advancement or improvement in the Utes, this has been an eventful year at these agencies" (referring to the Unitah and Ouray Agencies).

He further says:
"The work of civilizing the Utes will be slow under any condition of things. It will take more than one generation under the most favorable circumstances, and with the best means that can possibly be devised, to elevate them to a satisfactory standard of civilization."

Wm. A. McKewen, clerk in charge of the Ouray Agency, in his report of date August 14, 1886, says:
"These Indians are what is known as blanket Indians. As a rule are lazy, shiftless, vicious, and densely ignorant.

* * * * * * * * * * *

"I have yet to see one Indian (speaking of the Utes) who professes or has any religious beliefs or any idea of the Creator and the great truths of Christianity. The missionary and religious

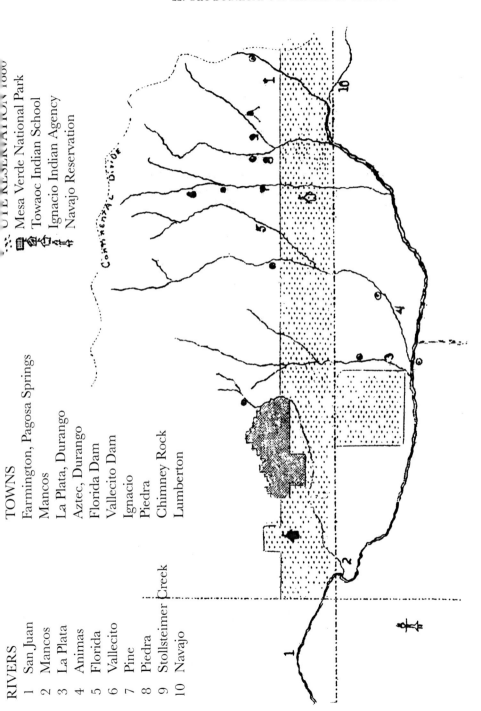

RIVERS

1 San Juan
2 Mancos
3 La Plata
4 Animas
5 Florida
6 Vallecito
7 Pine
8 Piedra
9 Stollsteimer Creek
10 Navajo

TOWNS

Farmington, Pagosa Springs
Mancos
La Plata, Durango
Aztec, Durango
Florida Dam
Vallecito Dam
Ignacio
Piedra
Chimney Rock
Lumberton

UTE RESERVATION 1880

Mesa Verde National Park
Towaoc Indian School
Ignacio Indian Agency
Navajo Reservation

societies of the East have sadly neglected these Utes, or do not know of this very fertile field for their labor."

These statements are true of every branch of the Ute tribe, wherever located, and are as true now as they were in 1886.

For the past thirty years every treaty or agreement which has been negotiated with the Utes has offered a liberal bounty to every one of them who would take land in severalty and engaged in agriculture. To the present date not one has accepted the offer.

The pastors of the churches of the City of Durango, Colorado, which is in the immediate vicinity of this reservation, in a public letter, of date of Dec. 9, 1889, say on this subject:

"One remedy proposed for all these evils is to give these Indians land in severalty, and then compel them to support themselves. This we believe the ultimate solution of this difficult problem, and is the end to which the efforts of Government should be directed. But this cannot be accomplished in a day or a year or a single generation, and those best acquainted with the Southern Utes are convinced that such a step now would only defeat the purpose of Government. These Indians have no disposition to farm, nor will they ever engage in it till their taste and habits are modified, and this can only be affected by education and civilization. This requires time. Past attempts to teach them to farm have been invariably unsuccessful, nor can this which we desire to see be accomplished under the present system, or with much hopes of success on the present reservation.

"Another fatal objection to giving these people lands in severalty now and especially of placing them and the whites on alternate sections, is the peculiar temptation to which they will be subjected. Everyone knows the peculiar passion of Indians for strong drink, and this is particularly the case with the Southern Utes. Under the present restrictions whiskey cannot be kept away from them, and were they and the whites settled on this or any other land the evil would be augmented a thousand fold. The whole United States Army could scarcely keep liquor away from them. In the first place, none but men of the worst character, those who would make gain out of the appetites and weaknesses of the Indians, would consent to such an arrangement. The Indians themselves see this danger and make this a strong objection to such a plan. Buckskin Charley, one of the Chiefs, recently said that if this plan were adopted that there would not be an Indian left in three years. They would all kill themselves by drinking. This is probably the strongest objection to be urged against such a proposal and we, in the interest of these Indians, ask that it be carefully considered by their friends in the East. Save them from this kind of civilization if you would civilize them.

"It is our unanimous opinion that they would be far better off today had they never come into contact with most of the civilization by which they have been surrounded. The advantages of the proposed reservation in Utah have been set forth in the Commissioner's report. Place them there where they will be protected on three sides by natural boundaries and the Christian church will then have an opportunity to do something for them.

"Heretofore nothing has been done for their education and evangelization by the church for the simple reason that they cannot be found on their reservation. At present writing the majority of the males are on the proposed reservation in Utah."

This objection is entirely obviated, however, by the fact that in the last Congress, the House Committee of Indian Affairs, by the consent of all parties concerned, adopted an amendment to the effect that any Indian preferring to remain upon the present reservation and take an allotment of land in severalty should be allowed to do so. This amendment is or will be incorporated into the bill pending before the present Congress.

These Southern Utes have a natural inclination for, and are anxious to, engage in stockraising like their friends and relatives the Navajos, whose reservation they would adjoin if the present agreement be ratified.

Experience has shown that this is the first natural step towards the civilization of the Indians. As proof of this, one need not look further than to the history of the Navajos.

The bow is 42" long. Middle width 1" tapers to 1/2" at tip. Middle thickness 1/2" tapers to wedge at tip. Sinew backed the entire length, sinew bound at center and ends. Red paint at end and center. Original bow string was corded sinew.

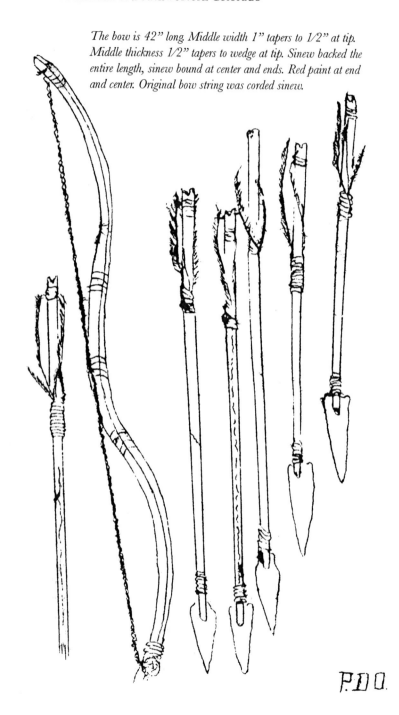

P.D.O.

Arrows are 25" long, pencil thick. Feathers at end 6 1/4." Three feather quills attacked at one end. Iron arrow point is 1 1/2" long, flat tapering triangle with long stem bound by sinew. Shafts are painted with yellow, one with red, and quill ends are individually stripped with red, yellow, blue and purple. One shaft incised with zig-zag marking. This decoration enables the hunter to identify and claim his kill.

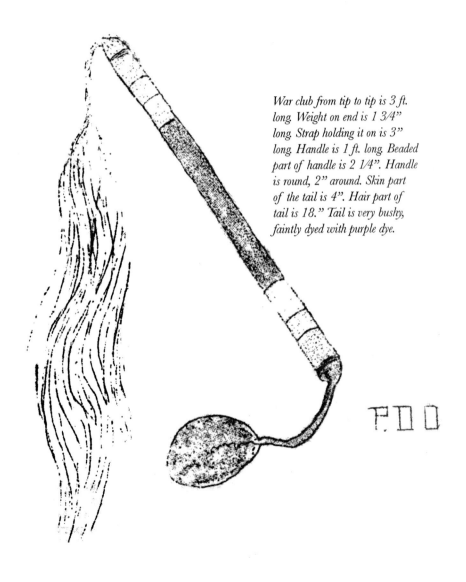

War club from tip to tip is 3 ft. long. Weight on end is 1 3/4" long. Strap holding it on is 3" long. Handle is 1 ft. long. Beaded part of handle is 2 1/4". Handle is round, 2" around. Skin part of the tail is 4". Hair part of tail is 18." Tail is very bushy, faintly dyed with purple dye.

They composed a very large and war-like tribe. A number of years ago they were effectively subdued by the Government, and being settled upon a reservation suitable for pastoral purposes they were given sheep, horses and cows.

Their agent, in his report of date September 1, 1888, states that they then owned 245,000 horses and ponies, 300 mules, 3,500 cattle, 800,000 sheep, 300,000 goats, and 500 burros.

Their wool-clip for that year was 1,200,000 pounds. Of this they sold to traders 800,000 pounds, using the remainder for the manufacture of blankets and clothing.

He further reports that they were desirous of building "better houses of stone and logs," and living "more like Americans, with permanent homes;" that their "demand for lumber, doors, and windows were incessant;" that the Indians themselves built the walls and did the work.

A further gratifying evidence of their improvement and progress is, according to this report, that some of them had begun to engage in farming, it being estimated that 10,000 acres were tilled by them during that year.

This agent further says: "The conduct of the Indians during the past year was uniformly good. The habit of industry is becoming more fixed. Their desire to accumulate wealth is fully equal to that of the white race."

Thus is the problem of the civilization of the Navajos, one of the largest and most savage tribes with which the Government has had to deal, being rapidly and peacefully solved.

So it will be with the Southern Utes, if given the same consideration and a reservation suitable to their wants and necessities.

THE PROPOSED NEW RESERVATION

Rev. Dr. Childs, of the Commission, who negotiated the agreement of 1888, visited the proposed reservation, and personally examined it. He says of it:

"This adjoins the present one and lies in the southeastern corner of Utah, with Colorado on the east, the San Juan River on the south, the Colorado River on the west, this river trending toward the east so as to make the reservation virtually a truncated triangle entirely separate from the rest of Utah. Practically it is more a part of Colorado than of Utah. It has an area of about 2,880,000 acres. A large part of this, along the Colorado River, is valueless for cultivation. The chief value of this reservation in its present state is for grazing. For years it has supported from 50,000 to 100,000 head of stock, the property largely of foreign capitalists. Naturally enough they have not been eager to give up the advantages of this land, the use of which they have had so long without cost.

But for this the Indians would have been settled here years ago. The average altitude of the land is from 1,000 to 2,000 feet lower than that of the present reservation. This gives it its invaluable character as a summer and winter range for stock, and explains the zeal of certain parties to keep the Indians off it. The amount of land capable of cultivation by irrigation, according to the carefully prepared statement of the United States officers, after the fullest exploration of the country that has ever been made, is over 150,000 acres. Against such testimony the judgment of men on either side who have no knowledge of the country except that gained in a few days and under interested guides is not to be considered.

The claim that the bill for removal gives 3,000,000 acres of roving land to the Indians is utterly wild, unless it includes the rights which they already have. Under existing treaties they have far more than this."

In March 1892, Lieutenants Robert R. Stevens and Charles G. Morton, both of the 6th Infantry, U. S. A. appeared before the House Committee on Indian Affairs, at its request and submitted a statement as to the proposed reservation of which each has made a through exploration and personal examination. As these gentlemen speak from personal knowledge and are wholly disinterested witnesses, their testimony should have great weight. Their joint statement was printed by order of the committee. The following extract from it should be conclusive as to the advantages of the proposed reservation.

"Viewing the country as an Indian reservation, the following points present themselves for consideration:

"First. The agricultural land that could be made available by irrigation from the natural water course would be sufficient for the maintenance of 1,000 or 1,200 Indians, allowing probably to each family 30 to 40 acres of fertile land, with a possibility of extending this allowance by the use of reservoirs to about 600 acres per family.

"Second. For stock ranges the country affords the greatest advantages of its alternating ranges and in the division which the natural rough features of country makes between these ranges.

* * * * * * * * * * *

"Fifth. The removal of stockmen from this section would prevent repetition of the troubles that have occurred between cowboys and Indians while the latter were off their reservation and traveling across the San Juan country.

"Sixth. The inclusion of what is known as the Renegade Indian Grounds within an Indian reservation would prevent the future use of that reservation as a retreat for lawless bands of whites and Indians, since such action would be in effect to place Indian police over that section of country, and it is a recognized fact that Indians neither retreat themselves to their own reservation in time of war, nor allow others in hostility to take refuge there.

"Seventh. An Indian Agent located at Blue Mountain could be easily supplied over the road from Dolores along the divide on the range, this road being open all the year round and being an excellent road of regular grades.

"We know no place remaining open in the west which would afford such advantages for an Indian reservation as the region above described both the present and the future needs of the Indians being considered.

ROBERT R. STEVENS
"First Lieutenant, Sixth Infantry
CHAS. G. MORTON
"First Lieutenant, Sixth Infantry

WHY THE AGREEMENT SHOULD BE RATIFIED

The present reservation is a strip of land lying along the southern border of Colorado and extending from the west line of the state eastwardly about one hundred and ten miles, and being only fifteen miles in width from north to south.

It is crossed by seven large streams having their sources in the mountains to the north and flowing southwardly across the reservation.

The valleys proper, or first bottoms of these rivers, are narrow and contain very little farming lands, but lying between the rivers and at an elevation of from one to three hundred feet above them, are large tracts of comparatively level "mesa" or table lands.

Within the reservation are some 350,000 or 400,000 acres of these lands, and these "mesas" extend southward into New Mexico and constitute the great bulk of the most valuable farming lands in that territory which lies contiguous to the Colorado line.

No part of this table land, either in the reservation or below it, can be farmed without irrigation, nor can any part of it be irrigated except by means of large ditches having their beginning in or above the reservation and extending through it, and requiring the outlay of large capital to construct and maintain.

The Utes are not farming or using their hands to any considerable extent. They do not even attempt to cultivate any of this upland. On the entire reservation they have about six hundred acres under fence. Only part of this is in actual cultivation, and even this is tended by Mexicans who rent the land of the Utes or are hired by them.

The government has furnished fencing, machinery, etc., and has provided a "farmer" at the agency to encourage and instruct the Indians in agriculture, but the results are not promising. They do not want to farm and very few of them are sufficiently advanced to do so if they were willing.

They have probably been as little influenced by the civilization of the Whites as any tribe of Indians that has had the same contact with it. They have no houses (except a few constructed by the government) or permanent places of residence. They live in "tepees" which they carry about with them, and it is almost impossible to get them to adopt the language, dress, manners, or customs of the whites.

They are inveterate gamblers and are very fond of whiskey which they get at every opportunity.

Their reservation lies like a string between the summer and winter ranges of the cattlemen and the cowboys are continually driving their herds back and forth across it. There is not sufficient grass upon it to keep the animals of the Indians.

Further, to briefly summarize a few reasons, the bill to ratify the agreement should become law:

First. Because it will open up for settlement many thousands of acres of rich and valuable farming land which at present are wholly unused and unoccupied.

Second. Because it will make it possible to profitably irrigate and farm the table lands in New Mexico which lie contiguous to the reservation and thus render productive these great bodies of land which cannot be farmed under the present situation.

Third. Because the opening of the reservation would encourage and induce the building of railroads and wagon roads into and through these lands and the territory adjacent thereto, and would encourage the development of the rich mining region of the San Juan and would materially contribute to the growth and prosperity not only of Colorado and New Mexico but of the whole west.

Fourth. Because the reservation interferes with communication between the settlements in Colorado and New Mexico for a distance of more than one hundred miles along the line.

Fifth. Because the very shape and situation of the present reservation makes it quite as unsuitable to the Indians as it is inconvenient to the whites.

The agency is not easily reached from the different parts of the reservation. From some parts of it the Indians have to travel at least seventy-five miles to get their weekly allowance of beef and provisions. They have to cross the several streams, and very often are compelled by the typography of the country to go outside their lines and on to the settled lands of the whites in passing from one point to another.

Again being so narrow and lying as it does between the summer and winter ranges of the cattle, it is pastured so closely that in the winter there is no grass for the animals of the Utes. They have to go off the reservation and into Utah or New Mexico to find pasture for them and every year the loss among those of necessity kept upon the reservation is very great.

There is little variety of elevation and none of climate. Some of us have been familiar with this strip for the last eighteen years. In eleven of that eighteen years the snow covered the greatest part of it to a depth of two feet or more for several months of each year.

It does not now and can never have good pasture and ranges for stock and consequently the Indians can not raise them successfully here. They can produce very little for their support unless we can presume that they can and will successfully irrigate and farm these table lands. No such presumption is warranted.

Sixth. Because the trespasses of the Indians upon the land of the whites as well as the whites upon the lands of the Indians, are a constant source of irritation and a menace to the safety of the Indians as well as to the isolated settlers, those trespasses cannot be avoided. The whites must pass over and often camp upon the Ute reservation. The only possible lines of communication between the settlements on either side for more than one hundred miles, lie across it. On the other hand, the topography of the country is such that the Indians could not pass from some parts of their land to the agency without going outside their lands and through the fields and enclosures of the whites.

They have also to leave their reservation for game and forage. The great majority of the white communities are friendly toward the Indians, and for the most-part they reciprocate the feeling, but there are those on both sides who are willing to give and ever ready to take offense, and the utmost endeavor of the great majority on both sides is not always sufficient to prevent a collision.

Seventh. The Utes want the treaty ratified. We offer this as one reason why it should be ratified, because we believe they ought to know and do know whether it would be best for them. They know their condition here, and they know the lands in the proposed reservation. They say there is as much farming land there as they can use. That they can raise sheep and cattle and can find pasture for their stock. That they can there hunt on their own lands without coming in conflict with the whites. That they can be more comfortable, accumulate more, and be in less danger than where they are – and we think they are right.

WHY AND BY WHOM THE RATIFICATION OF THE AGREEMENT IS OPPOSSED

The ratification of this agreement is opposed by a few cattle corporations, who enjoy free grazing privileges for their herds upon the public lands embraced within the limits of the proposed reservation. In case of ratification they would be deprived of these privileges, they fear, and hence their objections. Opposition from such sources, and based upon such objects and reasons ought not to have and cannot have any possible weight.

The leading officials of a society known as the Indian Rights Association also opposes the ratification of this agreement. They urge that the entire policy of the government towards the Indians is radically wrong; that reservations should be abolished; that the tribal relations should be broken up; that the Indians should be settled among the whites, upon allotments of land in severalty, should be made citizens, amenable to the same laws and possessed of the same rights and privileges as other citizens, and thereafter be left to their own resources.

The humane aims and objects of this association are in the highest degree commendable, but the summary method proposed to be adopted in lieu of the present Indian policy without any regard to, or consideration of the varying character and state of moral and intellectual advancement of the different tribes, is in the highest degree objectionable. It would, indeed, speedily solve the Indian problem, but solve it in such a manner as would shock the sensibilities of mankind. Left to their own resources, unprepared as are the Southern Utes as shown by the overwhelming testimony of all acquainted with the tribe, unable to earn a livelihood even if so inclined, they would quickly absorb all of the vices of the whites with none of their virtues, and become marauding vagabonds. The race itself as well as the tribal relation would soon be extinct.

Steeped in ignorance and barbarism as the Indian has been for thousands of years he requires long years of preparation for the responsibilities of civilization and citizenship, and this can only be attained, as shown conclusively by the past history of the race, by the slow and patient toil and labor of the missionary preacher, priest, and teacher. As has said Ex-Senator Dawes, than whom the Indians never had a better and more zealous friend:

"To take the Indian promiscuously, and put him on 160 acres of land and bid him to be a civilized farmer, and then go off and leave him after you have separated him from everything that is Indian but himself, from all the policy, all the law, all the privileges of an Indian; to clothe him with citizenship and commend him to obey your laws and seek his redress in your courts, and no other, and then leave him—if this is what you are going to do you would better leave him where he is.

"The first great duty is to fit the individual Indian before you put him on this land, and then he will take care of himself. He will never do it until that is done. The Government is not going to do that after he is a citizen. He must take care of himself then. The government of the United States does not take care of paupers; they belong to the States."

To the same effect said President Cleveland when waited upon, during his former administration, by a delegation of philanthropists urging some measure in behalf of the Indians.

"No matter what I may do—no matter what Congress may do—the only power that can raise the Indian is the power of Christianity."

In his message at the beginning of the present session of Congress, President Cleveland says:

"I believe, too, that the relinquishment of tribal relations and the holding of land in severalty may, in favorable conditions, aid this consummation. It seems to me, however, that allotments of land in severalty ought to be made with great care and circumspection. If hastily done before the Indian knows its meaning, while yet he has little or no idea of tilling a farm and no conception of thrift, there is great danger that a reservation life in tribal relations may be exchanged for the pauperism of civilization, instead of its independence and elevation. The solution of the Indian problem depends very largely upon good administration, the personal fitness of agents and their adaptability to the peculiar duty of caring for their wards is of the utmost importance."

In conclusion we beg to say that the insinuation sometimes made by over-zealous opponents of the ratification of this agreement, that the white people living near the Utes are actuated by feelings of hatred and animosity toward the Indian, and by motives of greed and rapacity are without the shadow of a foundation in truth. Had this been the case, the casual encounters inseparably connected with the condition of affairs existing for the last ten years, could easily have been permitted to drift into a race war, and, in such case, the little handful of Indians upon the reservation must inevitably have been driven off, if not destroyed by the overwhelming numbers of whites, by whom they are surrounded on all sides. The present reservation lies within the counties of Montezuma, La Plata, and Archuleta in the state of Colorado and is bordered on the south by the counties of the San Juan and Rio Arriba in the territory of New Mexico. These five counties have a population of at least thirty thousand whites, honest industrious American citizens, who are endeavoring to make homes for themselves and their families and to develop resources which will add to their own prosperity and to the material wealth of the country. This city, alone, lying within four miles of the northern boundary of the reservation and being the commercial metropolis of the region embracing Southwestern Colorado, Northwestern New Mexico, Northeastern Arizona, and Southeastern Utah, with two daily and one weekly newspapers, four banks and two large smelting plants for the reduction of gold, silver, lead and copper ores, has itself a population now of about seven thousand and does an annual business of many hundred thousands of dollars. This long, narrow, unused and unsuitable reservation stands as a Chinese wall, in the pathway to prosperity of these busy communities, and it is neither strange nor reprehensible that they favor a measure which will remove this great obstacle to their progress.

They seek relief, however, by no unworthy methods, and only in a lawful and peaceable manner, and appeal to you as their representatives in the confident hope and expectation, that you will carry out to its fulfillment the declared policy of the Government with reference to these Indians, upon which both whites and Indians had a right to rely as a promise, and thus subserve the best interests, happiness, and prosperity of both.

Durango, Colorado, December, 1893.

ADAIR WILSON
B. W. RITTER
RICHARD McCLOUD,
Committee

SOURCE OF
"THE SOUTHERN UTE INDIANS"
By
Helen Sloan Daniels

The late Judge Richard McCloud was secretary of the Board of Directors of the Durango Public Library for many years. The writing pens which were used in the final signatures of the commissioners were donated by Rev. Childs of the Commission, who negotiated the agreement of 1888, to Judge McCloud. The Judge donated the pens to the Durango Public Library.

Mr. Ritter was a friend of the Utes. When his home was the only building completed in that block the Utes regularly camped there. Mr. Ritter admired Chief Ignacio and often spoke of the fine spirit with which Chief Ignacio directed his tribe and his care for them in rationing and taking care of the sick. Mr. Ritter practiced law in Durango for many years.

Mr. Adair Wilson was also a lawyer in Durango pioneer days, serving with Judge McCloud and Mr. Ritter on this committee appointed by the Durango Board of Trade.

The Durango Board of Trade, Exchange and Chamber of Commerce have played their successive roles in the development of the San Juan Basin. "The Southern Ute Indians of Colorado" was a pamphlet printed by the *Durango Democrat.* Only this one copy has been located and mimeographing of the pamphlet was undertaken in order that the copy might now be spared constant use. A map of the Ute reservation in 1888 is of equal importance in reconstructing the picture of early Colorado. A map compiled, drawn and copyrighted by Emil B. Fischer, "Author of the Mining Map of Red Mountain and the Mining Region of San Juan, Ouray, San Miguel and Dolores Counties, Southwestern Colorado, 1891." It includes Plat of Mines at La Plata Mountains and Plat of Navajo Indian Reservation extended in Utah, Plat of Durango and Surrounding, Plat of Needle Mines, and Railroad system reaching Durango. The map is projected into New Mexico in order to include tributaries of the San Juan River.

A section of reservation was later withdrawn in 1888 to establish the Mesa Verde National Park. The Colorado Cliff Dwellers Association was formed for the purpose of furthering this enterprise.

Mrs. A.P. Camp tells the story of the part that was played by Durango Club Women. Mrs. Camp and Mrs. Boyle were active in this enterprise, even to the final climax of making the long drive to Navajo Springs, south of Cortez, to secure the personal consent and signatures of the Ute chiefs to establish the Mesa Verde Park.

The Ute chieftains had been summoned to the trading post for the occasion and after their consent was granted they staged a wild drunk, dancing and shouting about the store building all through the night with the terrified ladies momentarily fearing the Utes would further celebrate by setting the building afire. Happily this did not occur, but the journey was less successful than they thought because some legal flaw was discovered in the signed agreement which made it necessary to do it all over again. When the chiefs were approached a second time with the explanation of involved red-tape, they said that if the Whites did not know their own mind that they would not bother with them any longer. It was quite some time later that they were convinced of the desirability of continuing.

The present zigzag outlines of the park super-impose theoretical straight survey lines upon the rugged canyons and cause many boundary disputes to arise between the Park Service and Ute chieftains.

PRINCIPAL UTE LEGENDS

(Contributed by Mr. D.H. Wattson)

"Ute Legend of Creation," from the *National Republican*, year about 1921. By Ford C. Frick, under caption, "Indian Lodge Tales."

Since the Utes have been a mountain tribe, they have been influenced in their folk-lore by the majesty and mystery of the mountains which have helped to form their environment. We can only expect, therefore, that their first legend—the creation legend—should be centered about one of the great mountains which they knew so well and loved so dearly.

UTE LEGEND OF CREATION

In the beginning of time there were no mountains, no streams, no hunting grounds and no forests. In those days there were no red-men roaming the plains, no bison, no antelope and no living things. Even was there no earth, but only the blue sky and the clouds and the sunshine and the rain.

The Manitou, who dwelt in the center of the sky lived all alone. There were no smaller gods in Heaven—and he was the ruler of the sky and the sun and the rain; and the lightning and the thunder were at his command, and the sun shone and the rain fell at his desire.

But by and by the Manitou grew tired and lonely and wished for new things to see and new work to do. So he took a stone and whirled in around and around until he bored a hole through the floor of Heaven, which is the sky, and the hole he made larger and larger until he could look through at the nothingness beyond. And he was much pleased.

When he made a big hole in the sky and was able to look through then he took the snow and the rain, and this he poured through the hole in the sky also. With it he poured, too, the stones and the dirt from the floor of Heaven. And the snow and the rain and the dirt and the stones fell from Heaven into the great nothingness and the Manitou was pleased with his work.

By and by, when he had poured for days, he looked down and saw below him a great mountain which had been built by the rain and the snow, the dirt and the rocks. And far below the mountain he could see a great plain which stretched away and away as far as he could see—for there was a great quantity of dirt and rock which he had poured.

Seeing the mountain, the Manitou was curious to know what lay beyond and what wonder the dirt and the rocks had worked. So he made the hole then he stepped down from the floor of the sky to the summit of the great mountain which he had formed. When he had come down he found that the earth and the stones had spread out and formed the world, which was large and vast. But it was a work of bare rock and dirt and the Manitou wished for something to make it more beautiful.

He stooped and touched the earth with his fingers and wherever he touched, there trees sprang forth and forests were made grown with trees and shrubs. The sunshine which came through the hole in the sky which the Manitou had made warmed the air and melted the snow, and great lakes of water were made; and the water ran down the sides of the mountain and made the streams. And on the level land of the plains great lakes were formed and rivers flowed and seas grew, and grass sprung up and flowers and the world became very beautiful.

So was the world created, and it was a world of sunshine and warmth—a pleasant world where the rain fell on the afternoon of every day and trees grew, and flowers and shrubs. And the Manitou seeing it was very pleased.

Every day he came down from his home in the sky to roam in the fields and to rest by the side of the streams or in the shade of the forests—and the world became his playground where he rested when his work in the Heavens was done.

But at that time there were no living creatures, no birds and no beasts, and no bear and no wolves and no fishes, and no redmen—nothing but trees and grass and water.

By and by the Manitou became lonely and wished for someone to inhabit these lands which he had made so beautiful, someone with whom he could talk and play. So he created the living creatures and put them on the earth—but that is another story.

LEGEND OF THE BIRDS AND BEASTS

(The material for this legend comes from the Moache band of the Utes. It will be seen that this is closely related to the Ute legend of Creation. Buckskin Charley is credited with giving the story to Mr. Frick.)

Now when the Manitou had created the earth and the mountains by pouring dirt and rocks through a hole in the sky, he was much pleased with his handiwork. So he rested for many days and lived on the earth, and rejoiced in the trees and the green grass and the rivers and the lakes which his strength had created.

But by and by he became lonely and wished for some living thing to enjoy the beauty with him and his heart was sad, for there was none to share his treasures and none to whom he could turn for comfort and for pleasure. So he set about to create living creatures who might inhabit the world and make it more beautiful with their presence.

He returned to Heaven and took his staff, and with his staff he went back again to the earth which he had formed. From the small end of his staff he fashioned the fishes—big ones, of various sizes and shapes, and when he formed them he breathed upon them the breath of life and placed them in the streams; and when they were put in the water they swam away, and so were the fishes created.

Then the Manitou went to the forests and here he picked from the ground great handfuls of dry leaves which had been cast there by the wind. These he blew into the air and there they floated and flew, and wings and feathers came to them and from that time on the birds were made to live upon the earth. And from the leaves of the oak were the larger birds—the eagles and the ravens, and the hawk—created; and from the aspen leaves came the red bird and the jay. And each leaf made its own bird, and each tree its own kind, and the woods were filled with the music of the birds when they sang.

From the middle of his staff the Manitou created the beasts—the antelope and the bison, the rabbits and squirrels, the coyote and the wolf, and the sheep and the fox—and these he set down upon the earth also, and so were the beasts created.

But when the Manitou had made all these and had paused to rest from his labors, they straight-way fell to fighting and the big killed the little and the strong attacked the weak, and the rivers and the woods were red with the blood of the beasts which the Manitou had made. And the Manitou, when he saw the battle and saw the creatures killing and being killed, was sick at heart.

So he decided to create some other living creatures, imbued with his own strength and his own wisdom; and this creature he decided would be set down upon the earth to rule the others and to make the laws and the rules and to see that the beasts ceased their killing and lived in peace and harmony together as he desired.

So from the big end of his staff he fashioned the grizzly, and him he set down at the feet of the great mountain and gave to him strength and wisdom to govern the world. And the grizzly was master of all the others and interpreted to them the words and the desires of the Manitou.

When the Manitou had created the grizzly he returned again to his home in heaven and left the beasts behind to inhabit the world which he had created.

So was the creation of the beasts and the birds and the fishes and all the living things except the red men, who came later and who were born through the anger of the Manitou with the grizzly and his tribe. But that is another story of another time which is told.

THE DECISION OF DEATH

Now, when the Manitou created the Redman to rule over the world he created him in his own image and made him walk upright with his eyes to the sky—and he was not forced to watch his feet as were the beasts.

But when the Redman was created and had lived for years in the peaceful valley the Manitou found that he was too strong and too brave and that he had created too much in the image of the Maker of us all. So he decided that it would not do for the Redman to live too long else he would become as wise and as great as Manitou himself.

So one day the Manitou appeared to his daughter, the mother of the Redman, and to her he told his fears. And as a remedy he suggested that the Redman be allowed to live only for an allotted span of years, and that then he be supplanted by his children and his children's children until time ended.

But first he thought he would give the Redman a chance to determine how he was to live. And so, in company with his daughter he went to the valley, where lived the Chosen People, and he called forth the wisest and oldest chief of them all to be the judge.

In his one hand he took a buffalo chip and in the other a stone and with the chief and his daughter he went to the bank of the stream to make the test.

First he tossed the buffalo chip into the stream and the chip floated for a while until it struck the rapids and then it submerged for a little way and again it floated and again it submerged, until finally it disappeared from sight around a bend in the stream.

And so the Manitou ruled the Redman should live for four years and then die and remain for four years, following which he would again come to life for a similar period. And the old chief was pleased and accepted the ruling.

But the daughter of Manitou, the mother of all the Redmen, was not pleased and pleaded with her father that some other arrangements might be made. And the Manitou, who loved his daughter dearly listened to her pleading and agreed that there should be one more test made and that the results of that test should stand forever, and the method of the test he left to his daughter.

She, seeing that the Manitou had not yet thrown the stone, and thinking that perhaps the stone had some unknown magic, except to the Maker of us all, suggested that he throw the stone in the water.

The Manitou, taking her at her word, tossed the stone far out into the stream, and it fell with a splash into the water and sank out of sight. And thus was the fate of the Redman decided.

The Manitou ruled that each Redman should live in the valley an allotted span of years and that they should die and his body perish from the earth and should never more come to life in the valley.

But in order that the Redman should not be hopeless and forlorn he promised that those of them who kept the faith and praised the Manitou and his good work should live again in the happy hunting grounds above the Peak, where there would be no death and where there would be no war and no trouble. And so the ruling stood. The Redmen were made mortal, to die when their time came, but knowing of the promise of the Manitou they felt no fear of death. And so it is today. We all must die, but living well, live again in that great hunting ground, where all is happiness and peace.

LEGEND OF THE SUN AND RAIN

(This beautiful little legend is handed down by the Comanches and gives their version of the creation of the desert. It exists, in a slightly different version with the Utes and other related tribes.)

Many, many years ago—so many years that no man is able to count them—the god of the sun and the god of rain had a quarrel. Each insisted that the other was lazy and did no work and each was jealous of the other and declared that his own importance was great.

The god of the sun declared that without him the world would be desolate and that the rays of the sun were much more important than the rainfall and the water. And the god of rain insisted that the sun was only a minor god and that next to Manitou, himself, the rain god was the most important god in all the heavens.

So they quarreled and quarreled—these two gods—until finally their argument reached the ears of the Manitou himself, who called them unto him. When the Manitou heard the cause of their argument he was angered, and he decided that an example should be made of the two gods, in order that they should know their true worth to the world and to the people who dwelt there.

So he caused a test to be made and he called the two gods to him. First he turned to the god of rain and to him he said: "You have said that your importance is over-whelming, and that you are greater and more powerful than the sun and so this test will be made. And for six months I will set aside a certain section of land and there you will dwell and do all in your power to make the grass green and the crops grow. The sun shall not come near you, nor disturb you, until the six months are up. At the end of that time the sun god shall have his turn and when the test is completed then shall we determine which is the greater and which is the more important.

So the Manitou designated a certain bit of land and there the rain god went to dwell, and each day he brought the gentle rains to nourish the earth, and the flowers and the trees and the grass.

Finally the water rose and covered the ground and there was no sun and no warmth to dry up the earth and the flowers began to die. And the tribes who had dwelt there in the land were unable to live—and they had to move to other parts and the entire land became an ocean.

The rain god, seeing the desolation, became sad and repentant and went to the Manitou and asked that the sun be permitted to come in. But the Manitou declared that the task was not yet through, and so he sent the sun to the spot and ordered the rain god away while he made the test.

With the coming of the sunshine the water disappeared and once more the trees and the grass and the flowers flourished and the tribesmen came back again to their homes and everyone was happy.

But as the days went on and there was no rain, the trees and grasses turned brown and died; the flowers disappeared and even the beasts and the birds were unable to live—and died of thirst. And the land became a desert and the tribesmen once more were forced to leave and seek other spots where there was still food and water.

When the desert had been formed and the flowers and the trees had disappeared, then the Manitou called the two gods before him and to them he said: "O gods of rain and sun. The test has been made, and now you know the strength which is yours. You who are gods are only servants of the world—and together you bring happiness and content and prosperity. But alone you are as nothing, for in this world each must do his part to aid the other—and there is none who is greater and none who is lesser than the other.

In order that you may remember this lesson I shall leave the desert as it is—barren and desolate, a warning to all of you. And when next you feel that you are all-important, or that your work is better or greater than that of your brother gods, look you to the desert and all its desolateness and remember that only by working together can we bring happiness and prosperity to our red children who seek our protection.

The two gods, repentant, went their way and worked together, the one bringing the warmth and the beauty of the sunshine; the other the gentle coolness and refreshment of the rain.

From that day to this have they worked together—but the desert is still there as a rebuke from the Manitou to his lesser children—and if you doubt this story go forth into the southlands and see for yourself.

THE BIRTH OF PIKES PEAK

In the golden ages of memory and legend when all the world was new and fair, and all the sky was blue as babies' eyes and just as clear, the paradise of earth, wherein all was happiness and contentment, was situated upon the smiling slopes that rose to meet the sunset skies. In these days there was no mountain range, no land of eternal snows piercing to the heavens that made a barrier 'twixt east and west. Instead, all was golden with the sunshine of happiness and purple with the afterglow of peace.

Here lived the chosen people and over them was the constantly watching eye of Manitou, the creator of man and beast, ruler of earth and heaven. And the world was good to look upon.

The chosen people, roaming the hills, felt not the heat of summer nor the cold of winter for the seasons were as one. The trees brought forth their fruit without cultivation, and the vines their berries, and from the ground sprang up the luscious maize that the chosen ones might not wax hungry and lean. The streams teemed with fish, and the air with wild fowl, and the woods and fields with beasts that gave themselves up gladly to be a meal for man. In those days there was no war, and no sorrow, and no discontent, but man was willing to follow the rules laid down by the all-wise Manitou who governed wisely and well.

But by and by bad spirits came—weak spirits from the low-land by the sea—not strong enough to fight the chosen ones in open battle, but crafty in deceit and discontent. And long they journeyed through the land, spreading their lawless tales and turning each against the other, until no man was safe and law-lessness held undisputed sway.

Then the chosen race lost faith; they cursed the Manitou and wished him evil; they spat upon his image in the woods and defiled his name at every thinking breath. And bad grew worse, and soon their homes were broken and horror ruled upon the land, and the sunshine vanished and the snows came. The world was a world of sorrow.

When the Manitou saw what the evil spirits had wrought, he became exceedingly wroth. He stomped his foot and the rain gods came and swept down upon the earth and the waters of the deep were released and hid the land; and everywhere was desolation and death. And the chosen race, fleeing in fear from the rising flood, rushed toward the western gate that leads to Heaven bearing in their hands fragments of soil and rocks and precious stones with which to build elsewhere a better world. But the Manitou saw in their actions nothing of good or sympathy or repentance, but only evil and fear, and so he forbade that they should bring their worldly spoil to Heaven.

So the floods caught them and swept them into its grasp, and as they died each evil spirit lost forevermore, cursed the great and wise Manitou, and they cast their handfuls of dirt and rock toward the Heaven they mocked. And there they formed a mountain, vast in size, towering above the advancing flood and shutting off all view of Heaven's light. As the flood receded it left the peak, a monument of precious stones and gifts, marking the path to Heaven, but in its vastness shutting off all view of Manitou and casting its great shadow over all where once was earthly paradise.

So today it stands on guard against the further ambitions of man and beast. In years that passed the white man came and gave to it the name of Pikes Peak, in honor of their leader, who first saw its giant hand stretching above the clouds. But those of us who know the story of the chosen race, which was our fathers', still see in its great height a guiding mound that points the way to Heaven, yet shuts off our view and bids us turn and wait till we are called to do our penance there before the throne where sits the Manitou.

(This legend of Pikes Peak, most famous of American mountains, is told by Ute, Comanche, and Shoshone alike. It is reported, too, by the Araphoes and Cheyennes—tribes of a different family who know the Pikes Peak region and who, in all probability, had the tale from some of the mountain tribes. It is very beautifully told, in part, in poems by Ernest Whitney, who spent years with the Utes of the mountain region.)

THE BRANDED BUFFALO

The story of the Branded Buffalo was told by Buckskin Charley, head chief at the Ute reservation at Ignacio, Colorado. The story is a common one with the older men of the tribe. Apparently the hunting party found the strange buffalo in southern Colorado near the Spanish Peaks (Twin Peaks). The Utes, as history records, were natives of eastern and northern Colorado.

For many years the valleys at the foot of the great mountains were considered the home of the Gosiutes, and even the bravest did not venture far from the shadow of the Great White Mountain where dwelt the Manitou. To the east were great plains, barren and dry, and these were infested by savage tribes, who fought and battled to death.

To the south was an unexplored land, according to story, one of the richest lands in the world, but the fathers said, the southern lands were the home of great gods who made their home in the "Twin Peaks" and who would not permit a stranger to use their hunting grounds nor fish in their streams.

But when the white men came, the valley became quickly filled and the buffalo were killed and the antelope disappeared, and we who were the Gosiutes could not find meat to eat nor grain on which to live.

So the oldest chiefs held a council and the pipes were lighted and the grave words were spoken and the medicine men brewed their herbs for a great decision. And finally it was decided that a hunting expedition should be made to the southland, and prayers were offered to Manitou and a big party was organized.

And at that time I was a boy just big enough to join the warriors, but I had not yet counted my first coup, and I was to go on the expedition. And so the party started southward and we journeyed for eight days until we came to the great twin mountains in the strange southlands. There buffalo were plentiful and we camped for the night for the next day was to be the hunt.

In the morning, after we had made prayer to Manitou we started on our hunt and by noon we found the herd and the warriors on their ponies gave chase and many buffalo were killed. And the warriors rejoiced to see so much meat and every one was happy.

But when we came to skin the buffalo, strange things began to happen. For every one of the beasts carried a brand stamped on the shoulder and all the brands were alike, and there was no one who could read them or knew the meaning.

The leaders were frightened and no one knew what to do. And even the medicine men and the wisest chiefs were unable to read the strange brands or tell who placed them there, for there were no white men in the land, and no tribe that used a brand, and besides no one had ever before seen a buffalo that was branded. And the warriors were much afraid, and they said that it was the mark of the strange gods who dwelt on the Twin

Peaks, and that the buffalo belonged to them and that no one dared eat of their meat, else trouble would surely come.

So the party returned home, and the buffalo were left behind. Even to this day the secret of the branded buffalo is unknown, and no other warriors ever have seen them except us and we are Gosiutes. Today at Ignacio, where all the old men live, the story of the branded buffalo is told about the campfire, and the old men shake their heads for there is no one who knows why they came by the brand or the meaning of its strange character.

But they were branded for I saw it myself long years ago when I was but a boy and was on my first hunting party with my people who are the Gosiutes.

CONSOLIDATED
UTES

D. H. Wattson

Consolidated Utes

We live in a changing world and one of our biggest problems is to learn to adapt ourselves.

In the early days the Indian Service was a branch of the War Department, and the officers in charge of the operations in the western country were interested only in promoting peace between the Indians and the white and the Indians were given rations of food, clothing and other necessities to keep them contented. No thought was given to the future—to the time when the Indian must take his place as a self-supporting citizen and no preparations were made for that event.

When the Indian Service was established as a separate unit plans were made for the present. Accordingly opportunities were made for them to become self-supporting: sheep and cattle were purchased, and good farm land was made available. Since then the efforts of the Service have been directed toward teaching the Indians to make the best possible use of their opportunities. It is a well-known fact that when a man is able to get something for nothing, he not only does not appreciate what he has, but he soon stops trying to do anything for himself—he becomes pauperized. Accordingly, the giving of rations has been abandoned for those who are able to make a living, and there have been substituted greats opportunities for support.

The Consolidated Utes are particularly fortunate in that they possess the best grazing land in southwestern Colorado and the best farming land in the San Juan Basin. The opportunity to make a good living is here for those who have the ambition and the will to make the most of it, and it is a source of great satisfaction to note that most of the Utes have accepted

the changed conditions and are rapidly becoming self-supporting, respected members of their communities. There are still
a few, however, who are hanging back and hoping for the old
times to come again. It is for these that this article is written as
warning that the old times are gone forever; and that if they
plan to enjoy the good things of life they must cease looking
backward. They must use the opportunities available today for
making the kind of life they would like to live tomorrow and all
the days to come.

—Supt. D. H. Wattson, *Consolidated Ute News*, 3/15/36

CONSOLIDATED UTE AGENCY IN COLORADO
February 8, 1936
By Superintendent D. H. Wattson

(Report submitted to Mr. M. W. Cleavenger, State Director,
Federal Writers' Projects. Loaned to the Durango Public
Library by Mrs. Henry Hamilton.)

The consolidated Ute Agency in Colorado has jurisdiction over
two Indian reservations, namely Southern Ute Reservation,
consisting of allotted land and the Ute Mountain Reservation
which is tribally owned and unallotted land. In answering your
questionnaire we found it necessary to give two answers to
most questions. The Symbol "SU" refers to the Southern Ute,
the symbol "UM" to Ute Mountain and the symbol "CU" to
Consolidated Ute.

CU—the Denver and Rio Grande Western Railroad
Ignacio depot is one and one-half miles from agency headquarters. U.S. Highway 160 runs nine miles north of agency
headquarters at Bayfield, Colorado. The agency is connected
with this highway by a good graveled road. The Southern Ute
allotments lie in the vicinity of Ignacio, a town of about four
hundred people. There are no hotels on the Reservation. A
limited number of guest rooms and boarding clubs are maintained at the agency. Rates of club: 35 cents to 50 cents per
meal. The agency is twenty-four miles (a forty minute drive)
from Durango, Colorado (population 6,000), where there are

good accommodations. Reservation is open all year around. The best time of the year to visit it is during the summer or fall months. Best time of day is from 9 a.m. to 5 p.m.

UM—Towaoc, Colorado, is headquarters for the Ute Mountain reservation where there is a sub-agency. It is about sixteen miles south of Cortez, Colorado, and is three miles off U.S. Highway 666 on a graveled road.

SU—Chief points of interest: a. Pine River, which abounds in good trout fishing; b. Burials of Chief Ouray and of Chief Buckskin Charley, who died in May 1936, one-fourth mile from headquarters; c. Southern Ute Boarding School; d. Home of Buckskin Charley.

UM—a. Sleeping Ute Mountain near Towaoc; b. Mesa Verde Plateau to the east and Shiprock and Chimney Rock to the south; c. Mesa Verde National Park is but a short distance from Towaoc. (This park is bounded on the south, east and west by the Ute Mountain Reservation.)

CLIMATE: Delightful. Annual precipitation at Ignacio is 17 inches. Mean annual precipitation during the irrigation season or from May 1 to September 5, inclusive is 8.49", or 49.75% of the annual average total. The precipitation range indicates a high in 1937 of 22.67" and an all time low in 1934 of 7.2". The mean temperature for a period of twenty-two years during the months of June, July and August is 64.6 degrees and for December, January and February is 25.3 degrees.

SCENERY: The scenery in this locality is picturesque and scenic with broken mesas, canyons, foothills, mountains and a wide variety in flora. Elevation ranges from 5,200 to 9,000 feet.

NATURAL RESOURCES: Coal, small timbered acres of piñon and juniper with few trees of commercial value, grazing land, natural gas, oil and agricultural or land resources. (16,000 acres of farming land)

Ute population in Colorado: 834

Health statistics for the year 1935:

Southern Ute births	15
Ute Mountain births	<u>23</u>
Total	38

Southern Ute deaths	13
Ute Mountain deaths	<u>26</u>
Total	39

Two modern hospitals are maintained under this jurisdiction. These are well staffed and well equipped. A field nurse is employed to visit Indian homes and conduct health classes. As high standards of living are attained, the health of the tribe should be improved and the death rate should be decreased. Health conditions are improving.

There is only one tribe of Utes in Colorado, but there are two divisions of the tribe under this jurisdiction.

HABITATION: The present reservation boundaries make up a portion of the original habitat of the tribe. The Utes originally covered or roamed over the mountainous sections of Colorado and the northeastern section of New Mexico, and probably went a considerable distance in all directions from their habitation. Early records indicate a great number of Indian trails and considerable commerce or exchange of craft.

The Southern Utes occupy allotted lands in the vicinity of Ignacio, Colorado, while the Ute Mountain Utes live upon tribal land. Ute Mountain Reservation covers over 500,000 acres much of which is fit only for grazing.

LINGUISTIC STOCK: The Ute language belongs to the Shoshonean linguistic family. "Imported" Indians; No complete tribes have been imported, but a few individual Indians from the Northern Utes in northeastern Utah, a few Navajos from New Mexico have not been enrolled into the tribe, although, in a few instances, where they have married Utes, their children are on the tribal rolls.

STATUS OF THE LANGUAGE: The language has persisted with little if any apparent change. All of the younger Indians are bilingual, a form of Spanish. The Utes gesticulate quite a little to make their meaning clear in conversation.

GROWTH OR DECLINE OF THE TRIBE: Ten years ago, 1925, there were 785 Utes in Colorado, the tribal census of 1935 shows that there are 834 Utes—a gain of 49 or 6%.

Tribal per capita wealth:
Southern Utes: $3,500.00
Ute Mtn. Utes: $1,911.00

The Southern Ute Reservation has been divided into allotments; the Ute Mountain Ute Reservation is in tribal land, none of which is allotted. Approximately one eight, or 50,000 acres of the Ute Mountain Reservation. All tribal land will be used by the Indians.

There are no large Indian-owned stock ranches.

The hay and grain crops harvested by the Utes are marketed locally. Much of the hay and grain are converted into livestock. The livestock is sold in Denver Markets, though a little is marketed locally. Reliable dealers in Ute crafts are: Verner Helms Trading Post, Towaoc, Colorado; Ignacio Drug Store, Ignacio, Colorado; Taylor-Raymonds, Durango, Colorado; Gallup Mercantile Co., Gallup, New Mexico.

Indian products may be seen and purchased at the Intertribal Indian Ceremonial at Gallup, New Mexico, in August. Products may be seen at the Ute Fair held at Ignacio, Colorado, at Agency headquarters the last week in September.

We have a project planned for 1936 which includes the making and marketing of Pah-Ute baskets. Twenty-two women are to make twenty-five baskets each. Many more baskets were made and sold as a result of this project.

The Southern Ute Boarding School is in operation at Ignacio, Colorado. Enrollment is limited to 200 children, about 90% of which are Navajos. About sixty Southern Ute children attend Ignacio, Tiffany, and Bayfield Public Schools. The Ute

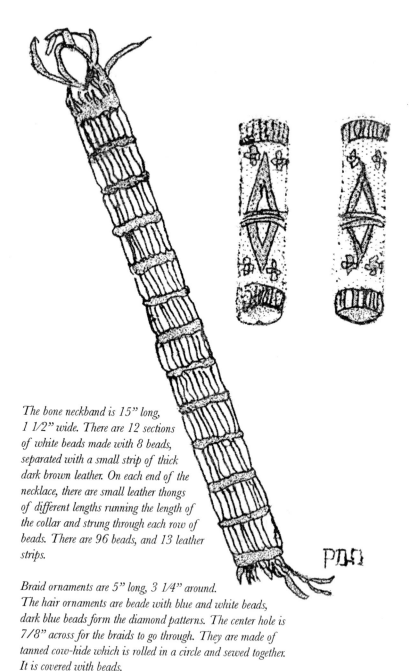

The bone neckband is 15" long,
1 1/2" wide. There are 12 sections
of white beads made with 8 beads,
separated with a small strip of thick
dark brown leather. On each end of the
necklace, there are small leather thongs
of different lengths running the length of
the collar and strung through each row of
beads. There are 96 beads, and 13 leather
strips.

Braid ornaments are 5" long, 3 1/4" around.
The hair ornaments are beade with blue and white beads,
dark blue beads form the diamond patterns. The center hole is
7/8" across for the braids to go through. They are made of
tanned cow-hide which is rolled in a circle and sewed together.
It is covered with beads.

Mountain children attend the Ute Mountain Day School. There are fifty in attendance. Academic subjects are taught in the public schools. These subjects are also taught in the Government maintained schools on the reservation, but the course of study is supplemented or augmented by manual training, home economics, and the study of Indian arts and crafts. Seasonable athletic activities are participated in. Those schools should hold great interest to the outsider. Extension work and demonstration projects are conducted by and given under the instructors. The field nurse conducts classes in health, hygiene, and child care for mothers and school girls.

WILD FOOD USED BY THE UTES: a. Wild onions, dug from the soil early in the spring and during the summer are usually fried, but are also eaten uncooked. b. Wild potatoes are found on Ute Mountain; they are very small. c. Fruit of the yucca plant, in the shape of bananas. They are sometimes called Navajo or Ute bananas. They are also roasted for immediate consumption, or they may be dried, to preserve them for future use, by sun-drying. d. Service berries grow on some parts of both reservations. Often dried and kept for winter when it is stewed when desired for use. e. Choke cherries are picked the latter part of August to mid September. They are dried in the sun spread out on a cloth. When they are properly cured they are stored away for winter. Wild vegetable foods play a small part in the present economy of the tribes.

Hunting and fishing play very little part in the present economy of the tribe. Some game is found on the reservation, however, the Utes have been taught to observe the State laws regarding seasons and procuring licenses. Deer, some grouse, rabbits, and prairie dogs are killed for eating. Coyotes, badgers, skunks, foxes, bobcats, beavers, and weasels are trapped or shot to obtain the skins. The white men's weapons have been adopted. Some fishing (for trout and suckers) is done on the Southern Ute Reservation but none is done on Ute Mountain.

SU: The Southern Ute family farms on an average of about forty acres. The chief crops are alfalfa, wheat and oats. Most families have gardens. There are about eighty cows on the reservation, although not all of them are being milked. The methods of farming are improved with modern equipment used. The Southern Utes own grazing stock, cattle and sheep.

UM: Ute Mountain Utes do practically no farming, but are herdsmen. 453,106 head of livestock are owned by these Indians. This reservation contains both summer and winter range.

SU: Most cooking is done over the stove with modern utensils. During the summer some of the cooking is done over an open fire out-of-doors. Others build a brush shelter and move their tables and other furniture and stoves out there and do their cooking and eating.

UM: Cooking is done over a campfire or a small camp stove. Boiling, broiling (of meats) frying and roasting are the processes used. Mutton is the chief meat.

SU: Indian corn is pounded into, and is used for, bread, but white (wheat) flour is preferred.

UM: No food is manufactured.

The Utes have a way of preserving meat by cutting it into thin strips, salting it, then allowing it to dry in the sun. It is placed on a line. When thoroughly dried, it may be stored for future use.

SU: The Southern Utes live for the greater part of the year in houses which are either of frame or adobe construction. These houses have floors, doors, windows and some heating arrangement.

Some temporary structures are built: A summer arbor is built of poles and covered with branches of oak, cottonwood, birch or willow. Some tepees are still used on the reservation. The material for tepees is of canvas. These tepees are built on the usual circular pattern. Twelve to fourteen poles are used. The fireplace is in the center of the tepee. An opening is left for a doorway and a flap at the apex for ventilation and chimney. Over ninety percent of the Southern Utes live in modern dwellings, so-called.

UM: The permanent abodes of the Ute Mountain Utes are for the most part tents. A primitive dwelling constructed of brush is used for a summer shelter. The Navajo Hogan is being adopted for a more permanent shelter. This is a circular house, with a dome-like roof, and earthen floor, and is constructed of logs and dirt, or mud. About five percent of the Ute Mountain Utes live in log cabins which have one or two windows and a chimney.

WORK IN SKINS: The production of buckskin is one handicraft of the Utes. The skin is of very excellent quality when tanned but the method has never been thoroughly described. The hair is removed with a knife or sharp bone. Sheep brains are massaged into the skin and allowed to remain on it for several hours as it dries in the sunshine. Much manipulation with the hands or pounding with rocks is required to make the skin pliable and soft.

BASKETRY: Ute medicine or wedding baskets are always of the same general design and shape—a nearly flat bowl shape, similar to that of the old time wooden chopping bowl. Although both names are applied to the baskets, the wedding basket and the medicine basket. Some Utes say that the wedding basket is slightly larger than the medicine basket and contains some yellow color. The shape of the basket seems to be particularly adapted to the use. The flat, shallow bowl is very convenient for mixing. The Utes, it seems, do not now use the baskets themselves, but sell them to the Navajos, who use them for mixing medicine and at a wedding ceremony for mixing and serving a ceremonial corn meal mush to the bride and groom. The Utes probably used baskets in their wedding ceremony long ago.

Willows are used in constructing the baskets, a heavy stalk being used for the inner frame work, and a more slender shoot for the weaving material. A well made basket is very strong. Beginning in the center of the basket a willow is wound about in some such manner as the spring of a clock. The rounds are woven together with pieces of split willow from which the bark has been removed. To make this weaving material, a willow is split in thirds, and the pith removed, immediately with a sharp knife or stick. The split willows are often half in the weaver's mouth or drawn through the mouth in order to moisten them.

Water Jug is 8" high, 9 1/2" diameter. Neck rim is 2 1/2" wide and flares out to 3" at top. Two handles are made of horse-hair woven into the side of jug. It is water proofed inside with pinon pitch lining.

A sore mouth is very often caused by this practice. A sharp awl is used in the weaving process.

The materials are kept pliable during the weaving process by soaking in water or burying in the sand.

The background of the basket is of cream color, or the natural color of the willows. The design is in dark red and black. Commercial dyes are usually used, although a native red dye may be employed.

WATER JUGS: The Utes make a practical container for carrying water. Willows are used as materials, but the outside of the container is covered with pitch from piñon trees. The shape is similar to that of a jug. Two braided horse hair handles make a convenient place for fastening a strap which is sometimes used for carrying the jug.

Weaving: None

Pottery: None

WORK IN WOOD: Very little wood handicraft is done by the Utes. One article made of wood, both useful and decorative, is the love flute. These flutes are covered with designs, either floral, realistic, geometric and are highly colored. A design may be carved or burned into the wood. A jack-knife is used for carving and a hot sharp object such as a nail or piece of wire is used to burn the design. These flutes are made of slender cedar sticks, and are two inches in diameter and 1-1/2 ft. to 3-1/2 ft. in length. The stick is cut in half lengthwise, and the center parts are removed, and then the two parts are glued together, forming a tube. Several holes are placed near one end so that different notes may be played. The blowing end is tapered off for a mouth-piece. A decorative carving, usually of a lizard, is made and attached near the mouth-piece. The flute is used in courting.

METAL WORK: None

OTHER TYPICAL ARTS:

a. Beadwork: A large amount of beadwork is done, the most common articles being belts, hat bands, arm bands, purses, rabbit feet, dolls, moccasins, gauntlets, watch fobs, cradle boards (beaded designs used to decorate them), beaded vests, neck ties, collars, leggings, and beaded chaps, also saddle bags. A small loom made of wood and strung with thread is used for weaving. Commercial cut beads are used.

b. Bone: The small sun dance flutes (Not to be confused with love flutes) are made of eagle bones.

c. Quills: A little porcupine quill work is still carried on, but the art is almost forgotten.

d. Feather work: Some magnificent war bonnets are made with eagle feathers. For these bonnets the tail feathers of the eagle are used and they must be twelve in number which are sewed together. A tam-like cap made from some cotton fabric is used for a crown. To this the feathers are firmly sewed. A short beaded design is used to cover the forehead. To the crown a few scattered feathers are sewed so as not to reveal the plain crown. Near the part of the headdress which hangs above the ears, weasel tails may be hung. Feather fans are made also. These are used during dances. A few feathers are used to decorate other ceremonial articles, such as arm bands and shields.

SU—Buckskin Charley, or Charles Buck is the head chief for the Southern Utes, he was selected by former Chief Ouray and has held office since 1884. His office is not hereditary. The second chief is Edwin Cloud, selected by the tribe.

Buckskin Charley is quite an old man, being now about ninety-five. He is short and heavy set. He wears a mustache.

(Note: Buckskin Charley died in May of 1936.)

UM—John Miller is head chief for the Weminuche or Ute Mountain Utes. He has served as chief since 1913. He is about medium height, rather heavy set and wears his hair in long braids. He is about seventy years old.

(Note: Chief John Miller died in 1936.)

The Southern Utes have prepared a Constitution and Bylaws which were recently adopted by vote of the legal voters of the tribe. The Constitution provides for a governing body, defines the jurisdiction of the Council, defines membership, provides for organization of a tribal Council, describes powers of the council and makes provision for conducting all business relating to the tribe. "All its meetings shall be public to the

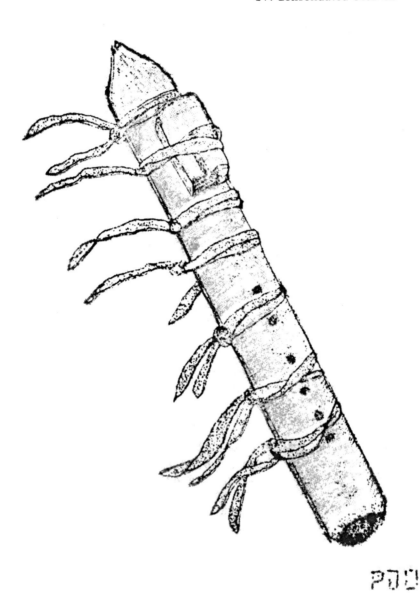

Flute is 17 1/2" long, 4 1/4" around. There are seven buckskin strings wrapped around it. Holes are carved on top. Above the holes is some type of flower painted on the wood. The flute is made of two separate pieces of wood which are rounded to a half circle, the center is hollowed out, then the pieces have been glued together with pitch. There is a small piece of wood which is glued on with pinon.

Indians and the United States Government representatives and may be approved by the Secretary of the Interior in order to be legal."

The Southern Ute Constitution provides for the establishment of a tribal court upon the reservation. This court has not yet been set up.

There is no evidence at the present time of clan survival.

The phratry, or brotherhoods of clans, does not exist.

In most of the families descent is reckoned from the father. In a few instances where the father had only one name, the children have taken the mother's name.

There is more individual life or family life than group life. The farmers and farm life of the Southern Utes and the life in widely scattered camps of the Ute Mountain Utes make very much group life impractical. The Utes, however, are very gregarious and enjoy each others' company when the opportunity permits them to meet. The Sun Dance and the Bear Dance afford them a chance to assemble.

Up to, and including the present time, most of the affairs pertaining to the tribe are handled through the superintendent's office.

The community meeting places are at the agency and sub-agency headquarters where the Councils meet.

There are no social fraternities.

The Southern Utes hold an annual fair and rodeo sponsored by the agency staff each year, on the last Saturday and Sunday in September. Some of those Indians also attend the Inter-Tribal Indian Ceremonial at Gallup, New Mexico, on the last Wednesday, Thursday and Friday in August.

Other activities shared in common:

Ceremonials:

BEAR DANCE: This is held in late May or early June. It is supposed to usher in the spring and signifies the time when the bear comes from his winter hibernation. It was formerly celebrated about the last week in March, but has been changed until later in order not to conflict with the spring farm work.

THE SUN DANCE: This is held in mid-July. It is a ceremony of sun-worship. (We believe that these Ute ceremonies are losing their significance and esteem with which they were once celebrated.)

The concept of individual ownership of property has practically replaced the communal ownership on the Southern Ute Reservation, but on the Ute Mountain Reservation land is owned as a tribal unit.

Functional ownership seems to have survived.

There is an ownership of functions. Only Utes participate in the Sun Dance rituals, but all visitors seem to take part in the Bear Dance.

Some of the property of the deceased may be buried with the corpse, burned or otherwise destroyed. Some of the deceased's personal effects may be given away. Land or other real property is inherited according to state law.

Both tribal and civil law marriage customs prevail. The new Constitution states: "All marriages in the future shall be in accordance with state law." In the past many Utes, when tiring of a mate, would go to live with another spouse without the benefits of a marriage ceremony.

The tribe has traditional songs. They may best be heard at the Bear Dance and Sun Dance. To our knowledge recordings have not been made. The Bureau of Ethnology, Smithsonian Institute has published a monograph on Ute music. (Densmore)

There is very little evidence of survival of Indian religion as far as the Utes are concerned. Designs do not seem to have any significance as regards their artifacts.

There is still belief in the powers of the medicine man, but this is decreasing. The title of medicine man is acquired supposedly through dreams. The medicine man believes that he has had a call from the Supreme Being. In the tribe he is looked upon as one endowed with great power. When a medicine man's patient dies, he does no more "doctoring" until so many days have passed or until after his patient has been buried.

The Roman Catholic religion seems to be predominant. It is estimated that from fifty to seventy percent of the Southern

Utes belong to this church. Perhaps a smaller percentage are communicants in good standing.

We trust this information adequately answers your questions, and it will be adequate for your purpose.

Very truly yours,

Signed: D. H. Wattson, Superintendent

SOURCE OF CONSOLIDATED UTES

By

Helen Sloan Daniels

When Mr. D.H. Wattson came to Ignacio to assume charge of the Consolidated Ute Agency we informed him of our need for and difficulties in finding authentic information concerning the Ute Indians. He promised to bear it in mind but never did anything about it until he received a questionnaire distributed by Mr. M. W. Cleavenger, February 8th, 1936. A copy reached the Durango Public Library through the courtesy of Mrs. Henry Hamilton who secured it while she was compiling material on an Indian Program for the Neo-Delphian meeting held in the museum room of the Durango Public Library in 1936. Mr. Wattson quotes the *"Ute Legends"* from a publication by Ford C. Frick in *National Republican*. Mr. Wattson's reply to Mr. Cleavenger's request was not used in its entirety in the Federal Writers' Project volume on Colorado, 1941 considerably shortened for condensation of material. We find it suits our needs to keep it as Mr. Wattson wrote it.

Mr. D. H. Wattson was the Consolidated Ute agent when the ration system was abolished. The recently completed Vallecito Dam will afford permanent irrigation as well as flood control for the Pine River Valley. Modern methods insure the completion of the agricultural program. Boys and girls are trained in vocational classes according to the best standards of today.

CHIEFTAN'S
MEMORIAL
MONUMENT

Chieftan's Memorial Monument

MONUMENT TO FOUR UTE CHIEFS IS DEDICATED
September 24, 1939

(From the *Durango Herald-Democrat*, September 25, 1939)

Yesterday afternoon, as a closing feature to the Ute Indian Fair, the beautiful stone monument to the memory of four great Ute chieftains—Ouray, Buckskin Charley, Severo and Ignacio—was formally unveiled and officially dedicated. Superintendent S.F. Stacher presided.

Mrs. Lillian Higgins, on behalf of Sarah Platt Decker chapter, Daughters of the American Revolution in well chosen and appropriate words, presented the bronze plaque of Chief Ouray.

Dwight Sexton, on behalf of Trujillo-Sheets Post, American Legion, the Legion Auxiliary and the Sons of the American Legion, reviewing in able manner the history of Ignacio, presented the bronze plaque of that great chief.

The plaque especially dedicated to the memory of Chief Buckskin Charley was sponsored by the Southern Ute tribes themselves, and Antonio Buck, son of Buckskin Charley, who is the present Moache Ute Chief, made the presentation talk. He made it in the Ute language, and it was interpreted by Dorothy Burch.

Superintendent Stacher, on behalf of the Federal Employees who sponsored the plaque to the memory of Chief Severo

made the presentation of that plaque, ably reviewing the history of Severo, whose son Rob, present Capote Ute chieftain, spoke in Ute of memories of his father. The chief of the Apache Indians was also in the speaker's stand. He spoke in his native Apache and the speech was interpreted to the assembly by Chief Antonio Buck.

The assembled chieftains of the various tribes, together with a few other selected Indian men and women including the now famous little "Half-Buck" and his but slightly larger pal, joined a special dance in memory of those four great chieftains to whom the monument was being dedicated.

J. H. McDevitt of Durango, delivered the dedicatory address, after which the assembly was dismissed in benediction by Rev. R. J. Hasstedt of Ignacio.

Durango's locally famous volunteer Dutch band furnished music for the occasion.

Following the dedicatory services, entertainment at the Indian fair grounds was afforded by an elaborate pageant staged by the Indian boys and girls. This involved an amount of labor in preparation for which great credit is due not only to the Indian students but to the teachers and agency employees, in supervising and making the elaborate costumes.

The Indian fair itself with its display of art work, agricultural products and domestic science processes was certainly an eye-opener as to what the Utes are really capable of doing. Superintendent Stacher and his able corps of assistants are

The feather cap is made of tanned leather. A headband is beaded with white, green and blue beads and is 1 1/2" wide and 24" long. 40 feathers sticking up straight are tied with colored strings of green and pink to keep them in position. The feathers are white and brown eagle quills 15" long, fluffed near the headband. Some yellow feathers are reddish brown. The feathers are strung in the middle with a thong of leather. At the back of theheadband a beaded panel of leather 8" long and 2 1/2" wide, tapering to 2" at the bottom, is covered with white, dark and light blue and red beads. Along the edge 26 little clinkers with pink feathers pinch. At the back a scalplock of human hair, brown 17" long is tied with a string.

entitled to a world of credit for the progress being made at Ignacio.

(The following description of the Monument and biographies of the Chieftains was obtained from an account written for the dedication, and later reproduced in the *Sunset Slope* of January 1940, with photographs of the monument and the chieftains.)

Superintendent S. F. Stacher lived at Navajo Springs in 1906-1909. An article in the *Colorado Magazine* of November 1940 gives additional information about life at Navajo Springs and adventures with the Utes. A photograph of Superintendent and Mrs. Stacher standing beside Ignacio (page 214) emphasizes a statement about the height of Chief Ignacio. Some superstition concerning photography was very real to the Utes, but this fear was not shared by Ignacio.

CHIEFTAIN'S MEMORIAL MONUMENT

Erected at Ute Agency, Ignacio, Colorado
In memory of Ouray, Buckskin Charley, Severo and Ignacio
By
S. F. Stacher

The Confederated Ute bands of Indians in the early days dominated a large area of Colorado, and history records many events, oft times of a warlike nature, during the early settlement and advent of the whites to the state. And for years there was ever present danger to the sturdy pioneers and prospectors. The last outbreak was in 1879 when a belligerent band refused cooperation with Agent N. C. Meeker, who under instruction had established an agency in 1877 on the White River, about six miles west of the present town of Meeker, with instructions to give every endeavor in the development of agricultural pursuits. This insistence was resented by some factions of the White River band which resulted in the massacre.

Since then the Southern Utes have progressed under the wise leadership of the Chieftains. And in commemorations of their Council, a memorial has been erected at Ignacio to these great men that the tribesmen may ever be inspired to follow in their path and ever be the guiding force in daily life of the generations to come. The memorial was dedicated September 24, 1939.

The erection of this memorial was made possible through the cooperation of the Federal Arts project of the Public Works Administration with Marvin Martin of Denver doing the art sculptural work for each of the four bronze plaques. The labor for the project was provided by the local Public Works Administration and Indian Service.

The red and white stone used in the masonry and enclosure was quarried four miles north of Durango, Colorado. The monument is eight feet square at the base, five feet square at the top and eighteen feet in height erected on reinforced base with a bronze plaque set in each face. The plaques were sponsored as follows:

OURAY
The Sarah Platt Decker Chapter of
The Daughters of the American
Revolution of Durango, Colorado

BUCKSKIN CHARLEY
Southern Ute Indians

SEVERO
Federal Employees of Ignacio
Colorado, Local No. 360

IGNACIO
Trujillo-Sheets Post of the
American Legion and Auxiliary
and S. A. L. Squadron from
Durango, Colorado

OURAY

Born about 1820 in Colorado, a member perhaps of the Uncompahgre band of Utes. Though later, due to his ability as a leader, he became the recognized chief of the confederated bands.

He was engaged in a fierce struggle with the Sioux Indians. His only son was captured and never was restored to the father. His relations with the United States government began with the treaty made by the Tabeguache band at Conejos, Colorado, October 7, 1863, to which his name is signed "U-ray" or "Arrow." He also signed the treaty of Washington, March 2, 1868, by the name "Ure"; though the amendment August 15, 1868 is written "Ouray." He is noted chiefly for his unwavering friendship for the whites with whom he always kept faith and whose interests he protected even on trying occasions.

It was quick action and firm stand on the part of Ouray that prevented the spread of the outbreak of the Utes in September, 1879 at which time Agent N. C. Meeker and other employees on White River were killed and the women of the agency were made captives. For his efforts to maintain peace at this time he was granted an annuity of $1,000 as long as he remained chief of the Utes. It was not until the time of Chief Ouray that the Utes were ever united as a tribe.

Ouray lived until 1880 and was considered an imminently great leader. President McKinley pronounced him "The most intellectual man I have ever conversed with." He directed his powers and energies to the task of solving the many problems growing out of the advent of the white man. His last illness overcame him on a visit to the Southern Utes and he died on the west bank of the Pine River near the present agency. He was secretly buried in the rocks about two miles south of the village of Ignacio. Approximately forty years later most of his bones were recovered and reinterred in the cemetery southeast of the agency and the grave appropriately marked. He died August 24, 1880.

Ouray early recognized the fact that his tribesmen must turn to peaceful pursuits or be annihilated.

BUCKSKIN CHARLEY

Buckskin Charley, or Yo-o-witz, meaning the Fox, as he was known among the Utes or Sa-pi-ah, was born in the Cimarron country. His mother and father were both dead by the time he was eleven years old. His father was a Ute and his mother an Apache, but he always lived among the Utes.

When a young man, he had many fights with the Comanches and Kiowas who were fighting the Utes over the good buffalo hunting country. In the last fight with the Comanches by the Utes at Agua Frio, Buckskin Charley was shot in the forehead with a pistol bullet which cut a feather off his war bonnet and would have fallen from his horse had not other Utes held him on until his senses returned. He carried the scar to the day of his death. The fight lasted all day and at night the Comanches ran away and the Utes followed them about fifteen miles.

When Buckskin Charley was about thirty years old, Ouray made him Chief of the Ouwache, also known as the Moache, band of Utes. They were living along Pine River.

Long before the allotments were made, Buckskin Charley, believing in a home, built a log cabin on the Pine River and began to clear and farm land which was later given to him as his allotment. He believed in raising a large garden of the things that his family could eat and then a crop of grain for his livestock. He had sheep, cattle and horses. The sheep and horses were herded on Mesa Mountain in the winter time.

Buckskin Charley's first wife was named Sally Buck. By this marriage they had three children, Julian Buck, deceased, Francis Buck, deceased and Antonio Buck, Sr.

Buckskin Charley served as Chief of Police for years at the Pine River Agency. He also served as Indian scout with the United States Army, joining at old Fort Garland north of Alamosa. While a scout, he went with the soldiers into the Western Navajo country. While a scout he killed a great number of antelope and the soldiers renamed him Buckskin Charley.

Buckskin Charley's first remembrance of Denver was seeing the white men planting trees and the next time he visited the place these rows of trees had become streets.

Around Pueblo and east of Colorado Springs was a great hunting ground for buffalo and there were also a lot of wild horses. Both the Utes and Comanches frequented this area; when they would meet a fight would result.

Buckskin Charley ably guided his followers in the ways of peace, friendship and agriculture, and sided in the progress of the Utes in the developing of fine farms. High grade sheep, cattle and horses are largely due to the foresight of this truly great man. He was loved and respected by all who knew him. He died on May 9, 1936, and is buried in the cemetery across the river from the agency, where he lies near the remains of Chief Ouray, and where appropriate markers have been placed.

By Isaac Cloud, who lived with Buckskin
for thirty-seven years.

BUCKSKIN CHARLEY
By
Nell B. McCartey

Buckskin Charley is the Chief of the Tabeguache band. Just how long he has been chief I do not know but have reason to believe that it has been a long time. When past eighty he was as straight as a ramrod. His charming dignity makes him a forceful character. He rode a beautiful horse and while riding him on a run he can shoot and bring down the elusive coyote. He is a fine type of Indian and one with high ideals. It was my pleasure a few years ago to have a rather long conversation with him. He told me that many years ago the tribes had lived in the mountains near Colorado Springs. They came to the San Juan country because the hunting and pasture were better here. It may have been in 1867 when the government made the first survey of townships west of the foothills. Buckskin Charley was then a young man in his early twenties. He told of many Indians fights but said that he had been friendly with white men. From all reports, this is true.

Buckskin Charley told me that if an Indian had used the poppy weed, a native opiate plant, or had left his wife for another woman he was not allowed to dance in the Sun Dance.

(This interview with Buckskin Charley was recorded by Miss McCartey in her paper "The Indians of the San Juan Basin.")

SEVERO

By Rob (Negerito) Richards, Son of Chief Severo
These things were told to me by my father, Chief Severo.

Severo originally belonged to the Moache band of Ute Indians and married my mother, who belonged to the Capote band, and thereafter lived with the Capote band and eventually became their chief.

He was born in the Cimarron country, and when twelve months old the Cheyennes and Kiowa Indians raided the camp, Severo's mother fleeing with him on horseback across the ice when the horse slipped down, throwing her and the baby. The pursuing raiders thrust a lance into his side, which wound healed under the medicine of the Utes. However, he carried the scar until his death.

The Capote Indians did not farm in New Mexico but after the Santa Fe country was taken from the Mexicans they were moved to the Pine River district and the agency was located where it is now. They had farms near La Boca, and Severo always urged them to raise crops as it was the only way for them to get along. When the farms were established the Capotes asked the government for a ditch and the government built them one. Severo urged his tribe to send their children to school to learn the white man's ways.

His words were always good. He advised me to go to farming. When Severo was a young man he had cattle, horses, sheep and goats enough for their own needs. In those days they had plenty of grazing land and each one took care of his own stock. In the winter time they moved south into New Mexico where there was less snow.

After the government came here, Severo had a few more things such as chickens and pigs, and he was put on a piece of land and had to stay there, and didn't have to fight anywhere as the government made the Navajos go back into their own country and they did not steal the Ute horses any more.

In the early days the Comanches and Kiowas would come over the trail at what is now Wolf Creek Pass and raid the Utes here and then there would be a fight and if the Utes killed any of them they would dry the scalps and put them on a high pole and dance around them. The Utes never went looking for trouble but would fight if their country was invaded.

Severo died March 24, 1913, age sixty seven, and is buried in the Protestant cemetery east of the Consolidated Ute Agency.

IGNACIO

Ignacio was a member of the Weminuche band of Utes. He sat in council in the early days with Ouray, Buckskin Charley and Severo, and was a recognized chief and leader of his band.

Nathan Wing, now living at Towaoc, lived with Ignacio for many years. Ignacio was given an allotment of land on the lower Florida River, a house and other improvements constructed for his use. Other members of the Weminuche band refused allotments and were placed on the Ute Mountain Reservation. Soon afterward Ignacio gave up his home on the Florida and followed to Ute Mountain, where the government built him a two-room adobe house located one-half mile northwest of the old Navajo Springs Agency.

During 1895 Congress recognized the services of Ignacio who was then designated as Head Chief of the Utes and gave him the sum of $500 in recognition of his services. The village of Ignacio is named in his honor. It is a pleasure of Mrs. Stacher and myself to have known Ignacio as we were stationed at the old Navajo Springs Agency, 1906, until March 31, 1909. He was the tallest of the "Chieftains" —about six feet in height. He walked erect and when he had occasion to talk in council he commanded attention. He and his wife received annuities and rations. He afterward was honorary Chief of Police with a salary of $10.00 per month. The association with this great man will ever remain with us.

He died near Navajo Springs, December 9, 1913 and was buried in some unknown spot east of this old agency. He was over eighty at the time of his death.

IGNACIO

Compiled by Lo Visa Lake Musser

In the spring and summer of 1879 there was quite an Indian scare caused by reports of the Meeker Massacre about one hundred miles north of Ouray. From early May until fall there was never a time when one could not see from one to a dozen Indians' signal fires burning on the hills around the basin. The citizens of Animas City, fearing for the lives of their women and children, formed a company of men and built a stockade on the west banks of the Animas River just south of the bridge. They also built a fort on top of the hill facing the river and a sod fort on the Gaines ranch in Animas Valley. General Sheridan, coming from Chicago to investigate the trouble between the whites and the Indians came in through Baker's Park to Animas City going on to Ft. Lewis then located at Pagosa Springs. This fort has been moved to Pagosa Springs from Tierra Amarilla in 1877.

When the General returned to Chicago he ordered troops sent out at once and in September ten companies, about five hundred men, under the command of General Ruell, a General of the Civil War, came in and camped at Animas City for two months. They stayed until conditions quieted down, chiefly through the influence of Chief Ouray and then left. Later General Pope was sent in and established a fort at Fort Lewis which they moved from Pagosa Springs in 1880.

Chief Ignacio also played an interesting part in the history of the San Juan Basin. A sub-chief under Chief Ouray he spent the greater part of his life in this section of the country and was never found wanting in his friendship to the white people. Chief Ouray had charge of all of the Ute tribes while Chief Ignacio looked after the Southern Ute, principally those in Southwestern Colorado and Northern New Mexico. He was born in 1828 and died at Navajo Springs at the age of eighty-five.

His was the interesting career, never failing to show his friendliness to the white people and many times preventing uprisings which were really brought about by settlers and the cowboys. Ignacio was not a chief by heredity. He was the son of a medicine man who had met with such marked success in his healing that he was regarded as an almost supernatural being.

One day, however, he failed to save the life of one of the prominent Utes and the tribe, forgetting in their grief, the debt of gratitude they owed to him for all he had done in the past, killed him. Ignacio, his son and a lad of only fourteen years happened on the scene just as his father was killed. All the hatred in his nature was aroused and springing on the council of braves who had slain his father, succeeded in killing more than half of their number. Then taking ambush, he continued to use his well-aimed arrows until he had killed practically every member of the family. When at last he returned to his fellows, he was a man to be reckoned with. His associates regarded him with awe and whatever his acts from that time on, all tended to increase this attitude on the part of the other Indians until finally he was chosen their chief. He was always just. He pacified the outlaw Utes, protected the whites when they were in danger of being massacred by the Navajos, and was never found wanting in his friendship for the settlers. His early youth was spent in Utah, his middle life on the reservation he took in exchange for the old, where he consented to go when a score of promises for the welfare of his people were made. It was the greatest sorrow of his old age that the white brothers had failed to redeem the majority of these promises. We have in our possession a pair of silver ear rings which he had worn a greater part of his life. These were given him one cold, stormy day during the fall of the year he died.

SOURCE OF IGNACIO
By
Lo Visa Lake Musser

Mr. and Mrs. J.J. Musser knew and understood the Utes. Our knowledge of Ignacio's boyhood has come through Mrs. Musser's story of the "Reminiscences in the San Juan." The Sun Dance Fan was a gift to the late Mr. J.J. Musser from the Utes. It is reputed that this fan is never sold and is given only as a friendship token. Her articles the Utes make have been loaned to the Durango Public Library Museum Exhibit and are herein described in detail.

Mr. E.E. McKean former superintendent at Ignacio Agency loaned his collection to the Durango Public Library. It is the origin for the material of the "Ute Medicine Man's Kit" described in detail in the Durango Public Library Museum Project Report for 1940, HSD.

Ignacio's earrings

The Durango Public Library has on display a sculptured stone, life size of Chief Ignacio. It was executed for display at the World's Columbian Exposition at Chicago in 1893. An imposing engraving hangs above the statue which reads:

LADIES OF LA PLATA COUNTY
Durango, Colorado

EXHIBIT: Bust and Pedestal of Pink Sandstone from LaPlata County:

AWARD

For excellence of a life-size bust of the noted Indian Chief, Ignacio, of the Southern Utes of Colorado. The subject of the bust is a fine, manly specimen of the Indian race, above the average size, and the likeness produced by the talented artist, an amateur, Mary P. Nichols of Denver is all the more striking because she used the finest grained, hardest, and most homogeneous of the red sandstone of Colorado instead of marble, the bust being of the natural color of the subject. The sculpture has been so well done that every feature of the Indian is strikingly portrayed and the expression is most lifelike and true. This

Exhibit is regarded as a production of rare merit, and time will enhance its value as it preserves for posterity a remarkably correct typical bust of the fast disappearing Redmen of America.

J. D. Inboden – Individual Judge

After the exposition was closed, the statue was sent to Durango to be presented to Chief Ignacio. He looked at it and said it couldn't be of himself, since he never wore his hair parted on the side. The library subsequently fell heir to the statue.

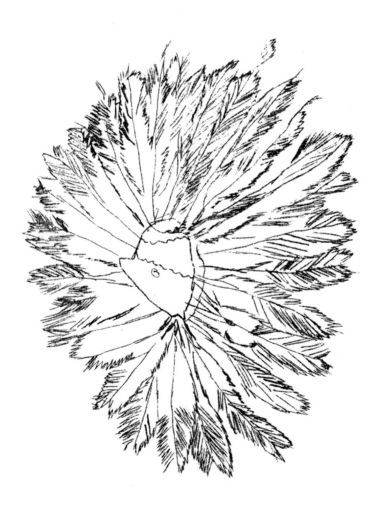

OUTLINE OF
UTE INDIAN
CULTURE

Albert M. McCall

An Outline of Ute Indian Culture

Albert M. McCall

The Ute Indians are classed as a Shoshonean stock or as belonging to the Ute-Aztecean language group. Physically the average Ute is rather short in stature and tends to obesity. They called themselves "Monts," meaning "one who speaks clearly."

The Utes were found in western Colorado, eastern Utah and extreme northwestern New Mexico. Their favorite habitat in Colorado was in the central mountain parks; in Utah they seemed to center around Utah Lake. In relation to North American culture areas, they spread around the point of intersection of California, Great Basin, Plains, and Southwestern influence and bordered on the north tribes of Plateau culture. The number of Utes probably never exceeded 10,000 in spite of the vast extent of their territory. This small number was due, likely, to the very limited food supply than to any other factor. The Utes were able to hold this area principally because of its impregnable nature; advance was even made, somewhat, at the expense of their neighbors probably after the introduction of the use of the horse. The Navajos were driven from the southern part of the Ute range in Colorado according to both Ute and Navajo tradition. They were not so successful in the east. Their relations with their neighbors varied according to political exigency. Generally, however, they were on friendly terms with the tribes to the west and northwest; Pah-Utes, Bannocks, Snakes, Shoshoni, on the south and

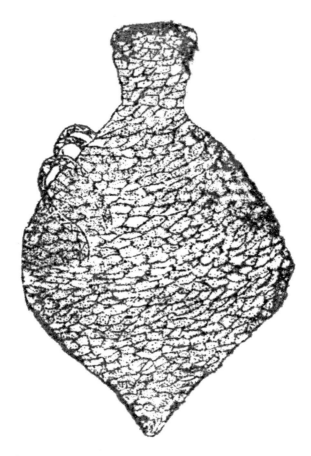

Cone water jug is 9" high. Around the middle it is 18 1/2." The neck is 5 1/2" round. The top opening is 1 1/2." It is coated with pinon pitch to keep it waterproof. It has two handles or horsehair which is braided.

Navajos were enemies as were the Apaches, save the Jicarillas, who were friends and subsidiary allies; on the north and east war prevailed with Kiowa, Arapaho, Cheyenne, Comanche, and Sioux. Sporadic raids were made on the sedentary peoples of the Rio Grande Valley and the Hopis. We might conclude from the number of enemies on the east and south that there existed a tendency on the part of the Utes to push eastward and southward; that the eastward movement was less successful than the southward, but undoubtedly held a greater attraction for Ute ambition, as the country would afford a larger and readier supply of food. Probably this movement was either begun after, or strengthened and accelerated by the use of the horse. Invasion by enemies, especially their eastern ones, often drove deep into the Ute country, as far at least as the Rio Grande del Norte. The raids on the Pueblos were not so significant as they were more in the nature of forays.

Where the Utes faced hostile tribes they lived in small village groups; to the north and east where peace prevailed they were found with the families roaming separately.

The physical region occupied by the Utes was varied; in their eastern range they lived in the Great Plains region, in their central territory were the high ranges of the Rocky Mountains to the west they occupied territory on the Plateaus. Because of this their living conditions were diverse; in the east, they were buffalo hunters, in the other parts they depended on small game, wild fruit, roots, and berries.

No doubt living conditions were uniformly hard; where the buffalo abounded a ready supply of food, there was constant danger of attack by enemies, elsewhere the food supply was very undependable. It is to be noted that the buffalo in the Ute country did not range as far west as they did farther north, not often going west of the Rio Grande. In addition, the Utes seem to have been very improvident, not being skilled in the storing of surpluses in the time of plenty.

Common foods in the west were yucca fruit, camas, tobacco root, yampah, grass seeds, pinon nuts, wild potato, service berry, chokecherry, fish, grasshoppers, and small game.

Agriculture, if it was carried on, was occasional and limited.

Meat was commonly roasted over the fire or jerked. Choke cherries and service berries were dried and ground on metates or pounded in mortars, as were the seeds.

The Utes lived in teepees of skin in winter and in brush shelters, made by placing brush over a frame of poles, in summer. Elkskin was in common use as teepee covering, but buffalo skin was preferred when it was obtainable. Teepees were notedly of poor construction.

The ordinary garb was a short skirt of bark or skins for women and breach cloth for men in warm weather, in cold weather the men donned shirt and leggings, the women in ankle length dress. Blankets made of elkskin or rabbit skin were worn in cold weather. No head gear was worn by men, except of ceremonial nature; the women wore basket caps.

The political institutions are very difficult to piece out. One item of Ute organization on which all writers agree is the division into separate bands or tribes; difficulty comes when they attempt to enumerate them. The Handbook gives thirteen; Dr. Hrdlicka three; Tabeguache or Uncompahgre, Kaviawach or White River, Yoovta or Uinta as existent and two extinct, Logup and Lubincariri. The United States government recognized seven in 1874: Tabeguache, Muache, Capote, Weemunuche, Yampa, Grand River, Uinta; at present six bands are given: Weminuche, Capote, Moache, Uinta, Uncompahgre, and White River. Dr. Hrdlicka applies the name to the Utes at Towaoc. A great deal of caution is necessary in applying any of these terms as it is more than likely these bands were but convenient groupings of a scattered people in a broken country—there was no stability in this relation. A man influential in a certain district was naturally considered the chief of a "band" by the white observer, and the facts were drawn as to distinctions of groups that never existed in the Ute mind. In common usage, today "Southern Ute" refers to those under the Consolidated Ute Agency at Ignacio, Colorado, consisting of three groups; one around Ignacio, another at Towaoc, Colorado, (formerly under the Navajo Springs Agency), and a small group at Allen's Canon, Utah, the modern Ute refers to them then speaking English as "Ignacio Utes, Towaoc or Ute Mountain Utes, and Blanding Utes, respectively. The "Northern Utes" are those living under the Ft. Duchesnes Agency in Utah and are called Utah Utes.

As it is with groupings within the tribe so is it with the chiefship. Chiefs seem to have been influential men in most cases, in other cases they were leaders in forays. The position of chief, taken in its first meaning, seems to have been, in a manner, hereditary, but probably that was due to the superior advantages enjoyed by the son of an influential man. In "Ute" history two "chiefs" loom out; Taiwai, and the later better known, but apparently less able Ouray. In one sense these men were not chiefs, at least as were other Ute chiefs. They were combined chiefs and war leaders, in addition they were able politicians and if we can be guided in the case of Taiwai by that of Ouray they were first class "bad men" that is they held authority by reason of their personal ability to meet out death to those who opposed them. Ouray in whose person were combined physical and mental prowess with a superior education was able to hold together a loose Ute political unity; if more were known of Taiwai, we would probably find the same true of him. The average, run-of-the-mill Ute chief was a man of considerable ability whose advice was sought by his neighbors and who tried to pass on his influence to a son or other near relative. The Ute "band" were the neighbors of such a man; three or less, thirteen or more, as the number of such men varied. Ouray and Taiwai were chiefs as we understand the word, exercising very real authority, but they were in no way typical—neither found, nor likely could have found, a lasting system.

Another common notion regarding the Utes is that a patrilinear clan system existed. The older Utes denied to Frances Densmore that clans had ever been known among them. Certainly no trace or idea of clan relationship continues among modern Utes. It is relatively safe to assume that there were no clans among the Utes.

Anyone desiring to lead a war party informed the chief, who assembled the men and explained the project. Those who wished joined together under the leadership of the instigator. A dance was held before the men set out. Bows and arrows were the favorite weapons. Examples have been known of the use of the shield. A cup made of a knot was carried by the warrior. Scalps were taken and they were carried at the end of a long pole or tied to the bridles of the horses. Scalps were given to women who had lost a son, husband or near relative in warfare or to a man similarly bereaved. The Scalp Dance was given on the return of the men.

BURIAL: Burial was by interment immediately after death in caves, arroyos, or shallow graves. The personal goods of the dead were placed with the body or burned. Those who had been abandoned as incurable were very likely not buried at all. There was a very real dread of the dead, consequently burial was as hasty as possible, consisting in the main of tossing the body in the most convenient place.

The religious ideas of the Utes were not highly developed. They believed in a bi-sexual deity He-She, and in minor creations or emanations of the supreme god—the Gods of War, Peace, and Blood. The God of Blood healed the "Sick" Earth was built from material in heaven, animals were made from God's staff, birds from leaves, the grizzly was the highest animal created. Man was born, immortal, to the daughter of God. He was made subject to death because of God's jealousy.

There were two types of shamens. The first, those who were supernaturally inspired, who were called to their profession by dreams and were in constant contact with their spirit advisers; who were the spirits of dead Indians, eagles, bears, birds, or a kind of fairy "the little green people." These medicine men's principal duty was to heal the sick which they did by means of magic called "pokantes." They never used herbs or other material means in healing. In modern times at least magic was made from material objects; a medicine man dug up a corpse to obtain the finger and toe nails to make magic a few years ago. Whether women were recognized as shamans of this class could not be ascertained.

Medicine men of the second class learned the use of herbs and other healing arts. Their practices have not been much studied. They successfully set bones and dressed wounds. In a modern instance a medicine man burned a young woman across the abdomen with live coals to assist labor in childbirth. Those considered incurable were abandoned. Men wounded in battle were washed at the Scalp Dance as a curative measure probably. The modern Sun Dance is wholly a devotion for health. Both men and women served in this class.

A head medicine man is supposed to have had control over the others; this is unlikely in view of the disorganized political state. Probably the individual who was considered, by the whites, as head medicine man was in reality the most influential and popular one.

There were few ritualistic elements in Ute religion. Each medicine man composed his own songs under the inspiration of dreams. Tobacco was ceremonially smoked. No trace is found of puberty rites, religious societies, or the use of the sweat house. In modern times, not more than ten years ago, the use of peyote was introduced at Ignacio from "Taos."

The distinctive musical instrument of the medicine man was the morache, technically a "notched stick with resonator." The resonator was originally a basket placed over a hole in the ground, later a drum was used. At present the drum has been replace by a large metal box. Large and small drums, bone and wood flutes were made. The wood flute was used in courting; the bone flute is used at times in the Sun Dance. The Ute was a prolific composer of songs, inspiration for which came in dancing. Songs were not believed to have any special effect in insuring success in hunting.

The marriage relation among the Utes is another point about which there are conflicting opinions. We quite frequently read that exogamy prevailed but if clans were not known then certainly exogamy was not. Again, some writers state that adultery was severely punished, this makes just a trifle of the "noble red man" tradition. From what can be learned today, there does not seem to have been a standard of sexual morality. The notoriously conservative Weminuche Ute at Towaoc are likewise the most notoriously unmoral. Hrdlicka observed this in 1900. The old men and women at Towoac have no particular sexual moral standard – at least as we understand it, while their middle-aged children make some effort to conform to the white man's code and attempt to get the young people to conform. Apparently marriage was rather casual, polygamy was allowed, there were no ceremonies, and when one or the other desired, separation occurred. Intercourse was engaged in by youths at an extremely early age. The marriage pattern, today at least, is the younger people frequently change mates, there is some exchange of wives, but in all this there is no general rule. As middle age approaches there is a tendency towards stability in this relationship—there is less changing, here too, we find no particular standard to which adherence is required or expected. As a prelude to mature life there is a period during which the children live with their parents, but are given freedom in sexual matters. While the mere fact of cohabitation implies marriage, perhaps, the assumption that institutional forms existed among the Utes is not born out of what evidence we now have. "Marriage" as applied to Utes should be limited in meaning strictly to cohabitation. Intermarriage with the Jicarilla, Bannocks and Snakes was very common.

DANCING: The distinctive Ute dance was the Bear Dance. Originally it was danced during the latter part of March. It is now danced in the last of May or the first of June. The purposes were: (1) to help the bears recover from the effects of hibernation, (2) to provide food for the living and spirit bears, (3) to charm dancers from harm by bears, (4) a mating dance. The erotic element is at present strongest. The dance is to the accompaniment of the morache.

The Turkey Dance and the Women's Dance were held at the same time. The woman's dance was adopted from the Shoshoni. Dancing preceded the war expedition, and the return of the warriors was celebrated by the Scalp Dance,

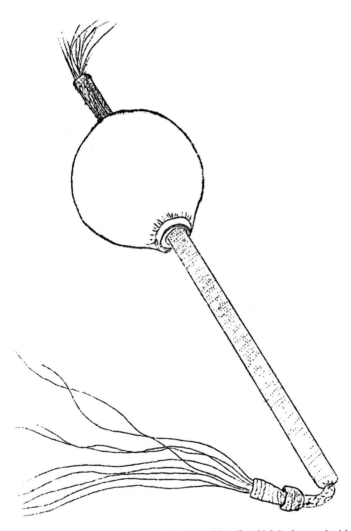

Gourd rattle is 24" long, about 1 1/2" around handle which is decorated with red, yellow, blue, white, pink, green and glass beads. The tassel is made of horsehair, dyed pink. Something inside gourd produces a rattling sound. Several leather strings of uniform length and thickness decorate the end of the handle.

followed by the Dragging Feet Dance, both being danced by men and women. During the Scalp Dance those wounded on the foray were washed, as were the bodies of those killed if it had been possible to bring them back. Other old dances are, the Lame, danced by women only and the Iron Line for both sexes. The latter was especially popular. Modern dances were the Sea Double and Sun Dances. The Sun Dance was first introduced by an Arapaho on the Northern Ute Reservation in 1904. It was not danced until a number of years later by the Southern Utes. Those who engage in it are assured of good health. Three days are given, at least among the Southern Utes.

Parades were held each morning when the Utes were camped together.

Common games were dice and gambling sticks, hoop and pole, ball juggling, double ball and shinny. Their addiction to gambling was conspicuous, even among Indians.

The Ute artist painted human, animal and symbolic figures on rocks and skins. Scenes painted on hides ordinarily presented dancing scenes, those painted on rocks showed the hunt and warfare. Hunting scenes were believed to have a magical effect in providing an abundance of game and success in hunting it.

Undecorated pottery of poor quality was made in limited quantities. Most of the pottery used came by trading with the Jicarilla Apaches and Pueblos. Basketry was considerably more developed. The material was willow. The most characteristic Ute basket was the water jug, an urn-shaped basket covered with a waterproof coating of pinon pitch. Medicine and wedding baskets were made to trade to the Navajos. These baskets are large and flat, the background is natural cream with decoration in red and black, some yellow is supposedly to be used in the wedding basket which is also slightly larger. The basket cap, an article of apparel for women, conical burden baskets, bowls and harvesting fans were made.

Ute bead work was very good. It is distinguished by the use of yellow, light blue, and light green. Porcupine quills were worked into designs. Feather headdresses were made in typical Plains fashion.

In making this short outline I have been very largely guided by modern Ute usage in conjecturing the condition of primitive culture traits. The customs of the Towoac Utes who are considered the most conservative and isolated of Utes cannot be ignored as a source of information and as a check on scattered observations gathered in former times. Of course due consideration must be given to the very destructive effects of the ration system and other factors.

The treatment of the Ute culture by most authors suffers from the attempt to be too general. The attempt to place all Utes in the same general plan. From the various environments one must expect a diversity of life. Utes who ranged towards the east partook largely of Plains culture, while those whose habitat was in the northwest of their territory followed a very different sort of existence. This difference is noted by only one author.

Next, having made the ideal Ute, the average writer attempts to fit him into an ideal plan, clans, exogamy, marriage ceremonies, and complex religious and political organization are all added unto him. There is no evidence that any of these factors existed.

In considering the Ute culture the position of the Utes marginal to four cultural areas is of the utmost importance. I wonder if we may not conclude from the close language relationship to tribes of the Plateau area, the Ute acknowledgment of kindred evidenced by free intermarriage with these people, and from the hostile relations with tribes to the south and east that the Utes advanced from northwest to southeast? His advance would have brought him first into contact with the California—Great Basin marginal area. Western Utes certainly retained that mode of life. Later must have come in contact with the Southwestern culture. Diffusion from here was rather small; pottery may have been introduced from this source. A small group of Utes at present found at Taos and as far as I can observe indistinguishable from the Taos Indians might indicate that there was rather more mingling than is supposed. I have not been able to learn how this group came to be established at the Pueblo. The wandering life of the Utes and their scattered and unorganized condition would preclude the spread of Pueblo culture. From the Taos case we might conclude that the acceptance of a large degree of Southwestern traits would lead to absorption into a Pueblo group. It should be noted that the use of the horse among the Utes was from the sedentary people of the Rio Grande Valley.

With the introduction of the use of the horse must have come a vast change which best can be understood by referring to Dr. Wissler's statement: "The horse was a great inciter of predatory warfare which must have increased the range and intensity of operations, thus intensifying tribal contact and increasing intertribal knowledge all of which favor diffusion. I think that we have here the key to the introduction of Plains traits, which so mislead observers who have limited themselves to Utes as they were east of the mountains. The poor form of the teepee seems to point to late introduction; the Sun Dance is very late. The effect of this new method of transportation must have been rather destructive to primitive Ute culture. The eastward drive was intensified, its outcome was never much in doubt, the Utes were repeatedly driven back with large losses; the further development of increased wandering; new traits may have driven off older ones, as a strictly modern example: The Sun Dance has tended among the Southern Utes to cause the abandonment of all other dances.

"The Ute culture can be regarded as being marginal to California-Great Basin in the west and marginal to the plains center in the east, there was no sharp line of demarcation between the two types, one shaded the other.

BIBLIOGRAPHY

PRINTED BOOKS
Chapin, F. H.
Land of the Cliff-dwellers
W. B. Clarke and Co., 1892.
Darley, G.M.
Pioneering in the San Juan
Fleming, H. Revell Company, 1899.

Densmore, Frances
Northern Ute Music
Government Printing Office, 1922.

Fremont, J.C.
*Report of the Exploring Expedition to the Rocky
Mountains and to Oregon and California*
Blair and Rives, 1845.

Hedge, Frederick Webb
Handbook of American Indians
Government Printing Office, 1919.

Howbert, Irving
Indians of the Pikes Peak Region
The Knickerbocker Press, 1914.

Hrdlicka, Ales
Physiological and Medical Observations
Government Printing Office, 1909.

Jocknick, Sidney
Early Days on the Western Slope of Colorado
The Carson Company, 1913.

Kroeber, A. L.
Anthropology
Harcourt, Brace and Company, 1933.

Kroeber, A. L. and Waterman, T. T.
Source Book in Anthropology
Harcourt, Brace and Company

ARTICLES
George Bird Grinnell, *Warfare of Plains Indians*
Clark Wissler, *The Influence of the Horse in Development of
Plains Culture*

PAMPHLETS
Denver Art Museum, Department of Indian Art, Leaflet
10: *The Ute Indians*

MANUSCRIPT
Statement to Mr. Morris Cleavinger, February 8, 1936.
Wattson, D.H.

SOURCE OF
OUTLINE OF UTE INDIAN CULTURE
By
Helen Sloan Daniels

Albert M. McCall enrolled in an extension course at the University of New Mexico and wrote this thesis. Mr. McCall was in the Durango Public Library while he was searching for this material and in gratitude for the use of the books and appreciation of the librarians' help he gave a copy to the librarian Miss Sadie K. Sullivan. We have numerous requests for information about the Utes and we find little to offer and that little is highly repetitious. Whenever the Utes are mentioned in reference or history texts the Meeker Massacre is always mentioned. The Meeker Massacre occupied four days in the lives of Ute tribesmen who had roamed the same territory for unknown centuries.

Mr. McCall found no evidence of integrated clan system. He is firmly convinced that there is no reason to believe they ever have had any. A contrary opinion was held by the professor who graded Mr. McCalls' thesis, herself a student of the Pueblo and Navajo cultures with highly developed clan system. She thought Mr. McCall had failed to interpret it.

We were very grateful for this paper, but the possession of it still did not meet our requirements of having something to distribute in response for information concerning Utes. Mr. McCall generously consented to allow us to mimeograph this thesis in order that it might be distributed for the use of the library, schools and club papers.

We visited Mr. Albert M. McCall when he was a teacher at the Pinon Grove School in La Plata County west of Ignacio. He pointed to the nearby dimly discerned trail across the mesa which early settlers say is the "Ute Trail" and is marked on many maps. Scattered stones bear witness to their camp sites as they still show teepee outlines.

Mr. McCall had many opportunities to learn of Ute customs at first hand, and he always emphasized the difficulty he encountered in making a wise choice of a neutral question which would give no clue to anticipate an answer. Dr. George Gallup and his staff were photographed in the "March of Time" series and the audience listened to the discussion which formulated a series of questions for his group to work on. At one suggestion, Dr. Gallup forcibly said, "No! That question is loaded." Mr. McCall assured us that the Utes were exceptionally keen in sensing your "leaning" toward a certain question and they are trying to be polite and not necessarily hypocritical when they try to fix up an answer that will please us.

From an extensive bibliography, we find that the same facts are repeated again and again, and Mr. McCall's contribution used here is a nice blending of published material counterbalanced with first hand observations at Towaoc and Ignacio.

SUNDANCING
BY
MOONLIGHT

By Helen Sloan Daniels

SUNDANCING BY MOONLIGHT

By Helen Sloan Daniels

Tires spattered gravel into space and beat a merry tempo into fenders. The world was a bowl of quicksilver patterns set in velvet shadows. The moon whose magic created this beauty hung at a disdainful height in the zenith—well beyond our reach and flattening our highest peaks into insignificance.

We saw the brush Sun Dance shelter from the ridge of the mesa and turned at the foot of the hill to work our crooked way through narrow ruts and sage brush which protected against bruised leaves with an incense of dust.

When we reached the brush enclosure we were efficiently waved toward a row of parked cars, each diagonally slanted so we could leave without disturbing our neighbors. (Just like a ball game and my heart sank; too much modernism would so surely spoil the picture we had come to see.)

Supper had been served to those inside the enclosure, drummers and singers probably, because the dancers abstain from food and water for three days and nights. Some friends who had arrived earlier had not been admitted until this food had been carried away.

We stepped inside the black coil of shadow and wood smoke by the north entrance and a large Stetson hat admitted us by taking our money (twenty-five cents) and lifting the edge of a blanket which hid the inside.

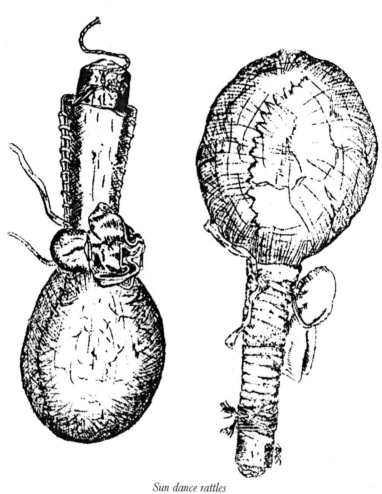

Sun dance rattles

Few were gathered as yet and the enclosure seemed much larger than the outside had indicated. A large tree trunk supported the roof timbers. Maybe it was a timber supported by imbedding in a posthole and maybe it grew there; it is too far from the river bed to be a native at root.

The left side, opposite the entrance, was filled with benches occupied by several men wearing large cowboy hats, but a few wore braids. They were grouped in clusters about the drums; we couldn't see how many. The women were squatted on the ground with their children in their laps. Long branches were held in their hands and waved in time with the singing and drumming. The moon was riding high and lit with a brilliant splendor three brush booths build along the outer support of timbers. This was roped off from the center areas to accommodate visitors who were permitted to go up to the rope. A bench was moved against the rope which bordered the dancers' pathway. Each booth served as a rest house for one dancer.

The central dancer was an older powerfully built man costumed somewhat differently from the boys. His tubby tummy was shirtless and a wraparound bright pink shirt was held snugly with a beaded belt. None wore braids. The boy at our roped-off side was a bulky, muscled youth, compact but not tall. He, too, was shirtless and his chest was covered by a ten hide presumably summer weasel with a large shiny ornament at the head of the skin. A thong bound it about the base of his throat, skin hanging flat and tail down. A similar hide was noticed through the opening of the booth where it was carelessly slung against a cross log.

All the young men had short hair cuts bound with beaded head bands and loosely wrapped red cloth with long white feather stuck up in the rear. The old man was gray-haired and wore no feathers nor headband.

Uniformity was evidently not desired. One wore a black shirt with beaded arm bands. I don't remember their foot wear, but I guess all were moccasined, couldn't see them above the shoulders of the crowd.

Rest periods were not frequent but seemed as much for the sake of the singers as for the dancers.

The drumming and singing began and the dancers shuffled out from their booths, one leg bent more than the other with an odd, hitching step, shuffling toward the center pole, looking steadily upward. This attracted our eyes to the top of the pole and we saw it hung with gaily decorated cloths like bright rodeo neckerchiefs. There was probably one for each, with no uniformity in the display. The moon arrogantly flaunted their bright colorings.

Upon the inner side of the tree, facing the dancers' enclosures and dimly outlined in the moon's shadow we could see a small doll or human figure with head, hands, and legs lashed by its waist to the pole. When the air cooled later in the evening they made preparations to build a bon fire, for breezes penetrated the loosely woven brush of the side walls. Disappointment followed for the flickering dash of fire only threw the little fetish into deeper shadow and so it remained. No questioning of visitors explained its meaning.

Perhaps there was some invalid whose hopes of health depended upon this ceremony of propitiation to the sun with its light and healing warmth.

Whatever the meaning of the little figurine on the center pole, the dancers' eyes never wavered from it to the audience. The dancers continued the jogging shuffle forward, then backing up. They sometimes came to the pole and sometime but a few steps from the booth. The central dancer stood alone by the center post, lightly tapping the tree, the doll fetish and himself with the feather Sun Dance Fan he held in his hand.

The dancers do not sing. Theirs is a harder task, a constant tooting of a bone whistle gaily tied with darting bits of feathers. The whistle, tooted steadily in rhythm with the steps, usually in unison, is accompanied by rawhide rattles shaken in the dancers' hands. The final measure of music finds the dancers standing at the doorways of the booths and the tones take on a pitch several steps higher than their former tootle, sustained for many seconds with such breath power that the feathers dancing

Bone Whistle
No. 3
Orange and brown woodpecker feathers and a fluffy white feather are tied by a
buckskin thong one inch from the mouth piece. An aperture is cut in the bone two
inches from the mouth piece. A small hole is drilled in the flared end of the whistle
tied with a gilt candy box cord to a purple feather.

Bone Whistle
No. 4
The mouth piece is shaped and reinforced at upper half of shaft with buckskin
wrapping. Reddish brown diagonal markings are scratched on bone. (Durango
Public Library Museum Project Report 1940)

from the end of the whistle dart upright and remain up in a final dash of rhythm of their own. Then after this surprisingly long-sustained note, all are silent. We stand there in an awesome hush.

The dancers step into the shelter of their booths and lean against the doorway. One flash of a match glows, we suppose they are allowed to smoke. One wraps himself in a light colored blanket or sheet, others loll on fallen logs which form seats. Not all dance every time, sometimes the old man is alone—although not for long.

During one of those rest periods, a small elderly man concealed under a large black hat which he did not remove, stepped between the drummers and the dancers and gave a long harangue in a high pitched falsetto voice.

It commanded silence from all, by now several visitors, many women squatted at the east of the enclosure near the entrance, a group of men near the fire. Those took no part in the singing. The only share of the women seemed to be a waving of their small willow branches with an intent staring at drummers and dancers, partly concealed from them by the huge center post, and concentrating upon the throbbing beat of the branches held upright, beating them lightly upon their knees.

Then all is quiet. The singers stop their chanting and drumming. The dancers retire to their booths. Men or women enter or leave the enclosure while the dancers are resting and the unit is definitely finished.

After a short time a dancer comes out from his booth. Singers and drummers join him and soon all are working up another strophe that ends with the high shrill note, the feather vibrating, the dancers still.

UTE COSTUME

By Helen Sloan Daniels

UTE COSTUME

By Helen Sloan Daniels

Careful study of old photographs reveals the Utes' costume.

A favorite type dress for the women both then and now is a cloth dress couched upon the shoulder yoke and sleeves with row after row of elk teeth.

Long ago George Catlin described this dress of the Pawnees. "The women of Comanche and Pawnee Picts (sic?) are always decently and comfortably clad, being covered generally with a gown or slip that reaches from the chin quite down to the ankles, made of deer or elk skins, often garnished very prettily and ornamented with long fringes of elk's teeth, which are fastened on them in rows and more highly valued than any other decors. Other articles may be couched in this fashion. A very beautiful costume was borrowed from Towaoc for the musical cantata given under the direction of Mrs. Henry Wilson of Cortez and presented at the 1940 CFWC District Convention at Durango. Attracted by the lustrous bands, we inquired about their origin and were told that it was made of badger claws. Natural curve and taper of the claws formed a circular banding about the neck and shoulders, metallic beads encircled each row and several rows are filled in this fashion, the glitter of the steel beads and the luster of the gray claws formed a most pleasing contrast with the dark cloth of the dress.

A few collectors have these dresses in their possession but this type is worn each year by Ute women at the Spanish Trails Fiesta in Durango. These dresses are worn on horseback and, since they are very narrow and pull up well above the knees, the women's legs are modestly concealed by brightly patterned fringed shawls almost long enough for the fringe to touch the ground on both sides.

The beaded headband with a feather inserted at the back is occasionally seen, but brightly colored scarves are frequently worn. Two heavy braids hang forward on the chest. The conservative braids are seen more often on women than on the men.

Utes are excellent craftsmen with buckskin which is used in various accessories. The moccasins are the most important article usually made with stiff rawhide soles and soft beaded uppers. Occasionally the squaws' moccasins have a wide straight banded cuff which protects their ankles. Moccasins made for sale to curio hunters are probably inferior in workmanship, they are scantily beaded and painted with a hideous shade of yellow paint. We have a small piece of Ute-tanned buckskin that is silver gray in color and as soft and plient as gray suede leather. It was tanned for Walter E. Weightman by Weaselskin, a Ute who lives on the Animas River about ten miles south of Durango. Samson Rabbit who lives south of Fort Lewis did beautiful buckskin tanning for Mr. and Mrs. J.J. Musser.

Elk and deer skin were the source of home and clothing. I have seen but one skin tepee, it was decorated with circular medallions solidly beaded with a horsetail attached to the center of the medallion. Before trading post cloth was available the women's dresses and men's suits were made of deer skins. The men's suits consist of moccasins, leggings, and long-sleeved shirts. It was the source of much annoyance to early mission teachers, when the Ute men cut the trouser seats out of store pants and reduced them to their accustomed leggings. A pair of leggings in my possession that are not illustrated in this booklet are made of scarlet flannel. Two straight strips of cloth are stitched two inches from the selvage edge and decorated with a four-inch band of beaded buckskin. It is stitched along the side seams and is elaborately decorated with three uniform triangles of blue and yellow upon a white background. Straps stitched to the top serve for belt loops. Before the coming of the trader and his beads imported from Europe, the buckskin suits were fringed and tied with hair or small tanned skins, decorated with paint or embroidered with porcupine quills dyed in brilliant colors.

Infants are carried in an elaborate cradleboard made of tanned buckskin with a curved willow-branch awning which protects the child's head from injury, a strip of cloth which protects it from light, small medicine bundles which insure its health, and beaded trinkets for toys. The Utes use the word "Papoose Board" but it is probably an importation the same as firewater. We do not know the word the Utes apply to the baby board. As soon as a child is able to walk and has outgrown the cradleboard the mother slings it within the folds of her shawl and carries it upon her back.

A long buckskin tobacco bag is ornately beaded and has a panel of porcupine quill wrapping on rawhide strips with a buckskin fringe. The upper third of the bag is not stiffened by ornamental beading and closes with drawstrings.

A smaller bag called a vanity bag is usually beaded on both sides; its lower edge ornamented with a narrow buckskin fringe to which small tin cones have been tied. Pendent cones furnish the musical jingling with which we associate Indian costume and dance and prompted our N. Y. helper, Mary Nestora Sena, to call them "clinkers" in her description. I know of no technical name for the metal fringe and consider clinkers an excellent choice.

Smaller bags of beaded rawhide are constructed in cones to carry awls, the sewing tools for buckskin. The thread is a slender strip of sinew. The stiff rawhide makes it necessary to wind the bead strands round and round. Another stiff rawhide with this technique are two cylinders through which hair braids are drawn. The braids may also be decorated with strips of silk, furs or colored wool.

A small case of special interest is a paint bag. The paint is held in a small envelope about the size of cigarette paper, and contains a brilliant vermillion powder, red ocher, with a smooth stick for application. The bag decorated with a narrow triangle of beaded buckskin with a string of blue beads, a brass button and a stone arrowhead attached. Arrow shape is slender, long,

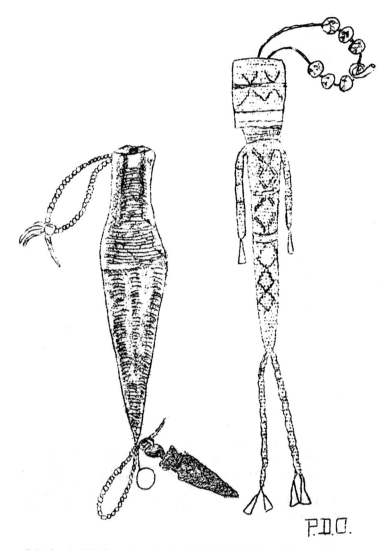

P.D.C.

Paint bag is 15" from tip to tip. Handle is 3 1/4". It is buckskin with bead
strings on bag part 8 1/2". The top part is 2 1/2" which contains the paint. On
the bottom there is an arrow head which is 2 1/8" long, a button and two little
1" strings of beads. These are tied with string.

Awl case is 17 1/4" from tip to tip. Handle is 3". Case part is 8 3/4". Log
part is 4 1/2". Clinkers at the bottom are 3/4". Arms are 2 3/4". Band part is
3 1/4" around. It is in a wedge shape. At shoulder it is 2 1/2" and tapers down
to 1/2". It is round at the bottom.

but not tooled as thin as the prehistoric points which we associate with this area.

Photographs show both men and women carry vanity bags. Men's costume accessories are more elaborate. The feather head dress gives the men special elegance.

One scalp lock of long eagle feathers is mounted on a beaded strip of buckskin, some narrow buckskin thongs on the underside can be tied to the head. Long cues made of tightly braided black horse hair forty inches long are hung from feathers.

We do not have a shield, but we see them carried by the costumed Indians in parades. A very beautiful one was carried in the 1941 Spanish Trail Fiesta Parade, a flat circle of rawhide with pendent eagle quills on about every third inch around the circumference. Early photographs show long spears and lances about eight feet long were carried with such a shield.

The traditional bow and arrow carried by the Utes is a part of their costume.

A war club is made of a stone covered with red horsehide attached to a hand piece with a three inch thong, reminds me of a burglar's blackjack. The stick is covered with red flannel beaded on both ends, and a white horse tail dyed with purple dye ornaments on the hand piece.

A token of brotherhood when Whites are inducted into a Ute tribe is the gift of a Ute robe. It is a generously oversized blanket of dark blue wool handsomely decorated with long strips of beaded bands four inches wide. The beads are attached to buckskin strips which are couched upon the blanket. When worn the beads fall upon the shoulders and arms. A slit is cut to insert one's head. Buckskin Charley was frequently photographed with his large robe gracefully draped around him.

The following description from the diary of W.H. Jackson gives a picture of the difficulties early photographers had while attempting to photograph the superstitious Utes. It appeared in the *Colorado Magazine*, November 1938, page 201. "Mr. Ingersoll, in his *Knocking Around the Rockies* (Harper & Brothers, 1883), mentions the incident at some length, having taken part in the first interviews with Agent Bond and Ouray about our purpose to make photographs. To this, as Ingersoll relates, Ouray "acquiesced heartily, promising to sit himself, and have his brother-in-law (I believe it was) also sit with all their best regimentals on. That afternoon, therefore, there was a large gathering on the veranda of the house of the Agent, the Rev. Mr. Bond, a Unitarian clergyman from Boston.

"Ouray ordinarily wore a civilized dress of black broadcloth, and even boots, though he had never cut off his long hair, which he still bound up in two queues—Indian fashion. But now he came out in buckskin costume of native cut, full and flowing, with long fringes trailing from his arms and shoulders, skirts and leggings, until they dragged upon the ground. These garments were beaded in the most profuse and expensive manner; as he gravely strode through the circle of spectators and seated himself in a dignified and proud way. His many medals flashing, he looked every inch a monarch.

"His wife (Chipeta) was that day about the most prepossessing Indian woman I ever saw, and Ouray was immensely proud of her. She evidently had prepared with great care for this event, yet at the last was very timid about taking her place before the camera; but the encouragement of her husband and assistance of Mrs. Bond, soon overcame her scruples and she sat down as full of dimpling smiles as the veriest bride. The doeskin of which her dress was made was almost as white as cotton, and nearly as soft as silk. From every edge and seam hung thick white fringes, twelve or fifteen inches long while a pretty trimming of bead work and porcupine-quill embroidery set off a costume which cost Ouray not less than $125.

"The third negative made was that of the brother-in-law and chief medicine man of the tribe whose dress was more resplendent than even his royal brother's being almost wholly covered with intricate patterns of bead work. He was a tall, straight, broad-shouldered fellow, and had not an unpleasant face, but it was thoroughly painted in vermillion and yellow—a bit of savage full-dress which Ouray and his wife, with liberal taste, had discarded. The most notable thing about this great sorcerer, however, was the evidence of prowess in war. The fringe on his coat, from shoulder to elbow, consisted wholly of locks of human hair—the black, straight hair of Arapaho and Cheyenne scalps that had fallen to his valorous share in battle. The heart he wore upon his sleeve was a dauntless one.

"We made good pictures of all three of these, singly and in groups, and had much fun out of it; but the consequences were dire."

During the spring of 1941 "Ute Agency News" appeared in *The Durango News*, a well written column reporting that social consciousness has been aroused. Membership and meetings of the Ute council are recorded. A group has been organized recently and under the direction of Sunshine Cloud Smith (could it be the Sunshine Cloud who, as a primary student, captured the interest of Miss McCartey?) is endeavoring to bring publicity of the most desirable kind to the ethnological problems of the Utes of today. May they be successful and continue to carry on such a fine beginning and make for themselves a niche wherein their racial entity yields pride and respect!

It would be an interesting study to trace policy changes under each agent from the early days of F.H. Weaver and C.F. Stollsteimer to the present Floyd McSpadden, as building of dormitory, gymnasium, hospital, and modern bungalows for the facility have been planned and then constructed. Perhaps this newly organized group may search out this interesting story and present it by and for themselves.

In intensive study of old photographs it is interesting to note the degree of adaptation to American "store clothes." A most beautiful costume of any age or time is that of the Ute Indian in full regalia. The fringed garment is enhanced with a fringe of scalp lock. The crested feather head dress continues with a feathered panel down the back, so many feathers may be sewn into this panel that the end must be looped up to keep it from dragging on the ground. Beaded panels, weasel and otter skins are attached to the bands above the ears, vying with the splendor of hair braided with otter skin. Colored beading of tobacco pouch, vanity bag, painted bow and arrows with the

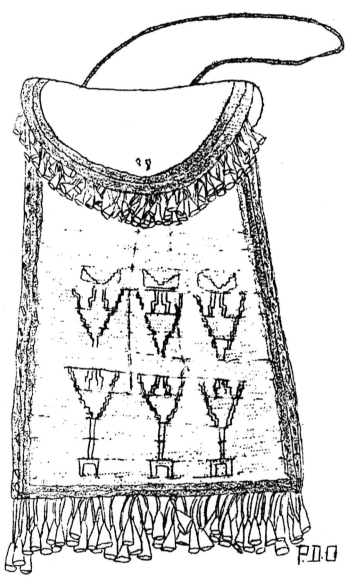

Vanity case is made from heavy leather which has bead work. Two strings of blue beads, one on each side, and a green stripe on the bottom. With metal clinkers on edge of bottom and on edge of bottom of flap with buckskin handle, which measures one foot. Case measures ten inches long. Clinkers are one inch. Base bottom measures six and one half inches wide, at tip measures 5 1/4". Flap part measures 2 1/2". Clinkers extend down 3 1/2".

quiver full of arrows, perhaps a long spear and a painted shield with pendant eagle quills.

His wife is no less picturesque in her shell- or elk-teeth decorated dress, with beaded moccasins. The costume of both man and wife is accompanied by sound effects created by the jingling of metal fringed beaded bags.

This costume was substituted with clothing distributed at the Agency by benevolent Uncle Sam. At each fiesta or county fair we see the Utes proudly displaying their colorful garments which still are treasured by them and that typify the pageantry of the life they knew before the coming of the Spanish Conquistadores.

Mr. Eben G. Fine frequently relates his experiences while conducting a party of Ute Indians to Boulder for the thirty-fifth Anniversary at Boulder. His experiences were recently retold at Ignacio where he showed them photographs taken in 1905. Some of his subjects were in the audience; the children grown to maturity were present with their families. His more recent account has been published by the Colorado Historical Society, *The Utes and the Boulder Semi-Centennial Celebration*, Number 2, March 1939.

During the Inter-tribal Indian Ceremony at Gallup, old head dresses and costumes are displayed by the Towaoc Agency.

A collection of photographs and Ute antiquities of historic value may be seen at the A. J. Utt Ranch at Bondad.

Memories of Chief Ignacio and the Old Navajo Springs Sub-Agency by S.F. Stacher are included in *The Colorado Magazine*, Number 6, November 1940.

Colorado from the American Guide Series, Colorado Writers' Project, Hastings House, 1940 publication includes many references to Ute Indians, Ute legends and Ute place names.

Traditional training has been eliminated by the attendance at the Government Schools and unless the young men are studying to be medicine men they know little of the background of the ceremonies. If they have been initiated into various degrees leading to participation in ceremonies such as the Sun Dance in order to become Medicine Men their lips are thereby sealed to secrecy. The Ute Warrior relegated the women's place in the home to the background, and it is highly improbable that the women received any instruction in these matters. An occasional woman may be exceptionally skillful in the use of native herbs in treatments for the sick and yet not be endowed with the religious significance which makes the place of the Medicine Man one of much power and authority.

A study of early photographs of Utes in ceremonial costume shows little divergence from the Plains Indian. It is interesting to note in our McKean collection that the floral patterns prevail in the beadwork of the Sioux Indians and geometric patterns are predominant in the Southwestern Ute collection.

Written history of the Utes began with Escalante. Their early territory throughout New Mexico and Colorado was gradually reduced by fights and treaties to their present boundaries. Mrs. Theodore Grabowsky was assigned to the Towaoc Hospital and accompanied by a Forest Ranger, took long horseback trips back into the canyons of Ute Mountain, visited scattered families with an intention of teaching health habits and treatments. Her description of Ute life differs little from those of Escalante.

The Government Schools teach the boys and girls farming methods. Their own customs fail to fit in with their present mode of living.

SOURCE OF
MATERIAL

By Helen Sloan Daniels

SOURCE OF MATERIAL

By Helen Sloan Daniels

There are few sources of information concerning Ute Indians. Many reputable authors assimilate information from the same source. A long bibliographical index presents exceptionally little data.

Our earliest written reference to the Ute Indians comes from a translation of Padre Escalante's diary in *The Catholic Church In Utah* by W. R. Harris and published by the Intermountain Catholic Press in 1909. Utah tribal or place names are spelled with many variations. Many spellings are noted for the tricky Tabeguache, Moache and Uintah. "Uintah" is apparently simple, but is recorded as Unitah, Uintah, and even Unintah.

A geographical item in Padre Escalante's story is significant. Where the Navajo River and the San Juan River join, Escalante named the resulting stream "Navajo" because it bordered upon the Navajo's country until it reached the Colorado River in southern Utah. Navajos raided north of this river and the Utes raided south, but they agreed upon a territorial division which was Padre Escalante's "Navajo River," which we now call "San Juan." Escalante was preceded by Juan Rivera for whom the San Juan was named, but we have no diary or account of Rivera's journey except for occasional references by Escalante. As mining claims were pushed westward, railroads were built, and land was farmed, the Utes were pushed westward and southward to canyons north of the Navajo tribes.

The Navajos were in turn forced into northwestern New Mexico and Arizona canyons. Although they were traditional foes, their mutual danger made them allies.

Dr. F. W. Hodge, director of the Southwest Museum at Los Angeles is a popular authority. His classic *Handbook of American Indians* was published by the Government Printing Office, Bulletin 30, 1912 is mentioned in every bibliography on Indians, and a standard reference. In discussing physical traits of the Utes he says: "Utes are short of strature with a strong tendency to obesity." Yes, and no. Ouray is a good example—both short and obese. The Utes are noticeably fat during adolescence and later in middle age (but aren't we all?). Now they drive autos and, as in the past with horses, never walk when they can ride. If you see a tall, dark-haired, brown eyed man with two braids falling in front of his coat collar, don't mistake him for a Navajo because he is tall and you believe Utes to be short and heavy set. Young men have appeared at the Gallup Ceremonial splendidly built, lithe and often handsome men, with heavy features and over-bearing manner decidedly not in a mood to accept friendly overtures as do the Navajos or Pueblos who welcome a chance for a conversation as an introduction to a sale of rugs or jewelry.

This aloof attitude of the Ute toward the white people is mentioned by all authorities. Their aloofness has continued throughout many generations of contacts with Spanish conquistador, Canadian or French trappers and American traders and settlers. They have not intermarried to the extent the Navajos and Pueblos have, nor have they allowed the children with Mexican blood to disseminate information concerning superstitions and legends. There have been some intermarriages between Ute school children and other tribes as they associate with them in the government schools.

A bulletin published by the Bureau of American Ethnology which contains much valuable information about Utes is entitled *Northern Ute Music* by Frances Densmore, and published by Government Printing Office, 1922. This is our source of information concerning music, games and songs. General customs are carefully interpreted and the book is highly regarded. It is based upon the Northern Ute tribes and just how much of this interpretation applies to the Southwestern Utes is not known. It was recommended by the agent at Ignacio, Mr. E. E. McKean, Sr., who believed it was verified in any particular that he had been able to test.

Another publication of the Government Printing Office (1909), is *Physiological and Medical Observations* by Ales Hrdlicka. This lists physical characteristics of Utes that distinguish them from Plains cultures.

The Land of the Cliff Dwellers by F. H. Chapin, W. B. Clarke and Co., 1892, is an interesting volume. It describes the converging canyons of Mesa Verde before any ranchers had penetrated the district. Utes are mentioned in this text appearing abruptly on lonely mesas, herding sheep or horses, aggressively warding any attempt of strangers to enter their camps. They worked for Richard Wetherill, and he seemed to have their confidence. Their conversation was bilingual. Neither group understood the other and interpretation often rested upon gestures.

Dr. J. W. Powell, First Annual B. A. E. Report, 1878, records the ability of Utes to use expressive gestures but considers it unessential since he had witnessed matters of importance settled while the Utes were blanketed and no gesture would be seen if made. The Utes have no early interpreter of lore such as Washington Matthew's accounts of study of Navajo life.

A very rare and delightful book is *A Frontier Life of An Army Surgeon*, by Bernard J. Byrne. His wife, Laura Lawrenson Byrne, published his diary in 1935 in a limited edition and graciously sent an autographed copy to the Durango Public Library. Dr. and Mrs. Byrne lived at the army post of Fort Lewis in 1881. His description of contacts with Ute Indians is colorful. Durango residents acquainted with Dr. and Mrs. Byrne are delighted with the authenticity of this book. Things didn't go well while quelling the rebellious spirits of the Utes. Many of the army regulations are revealed in these pages.

The Crest of the Continent by Ernest Ingersoll, published by R. R. Donnelly and Sons Co., Chicago 1880 is noteworthy in its illustrations as well as in its text. On the Ute council fire cover we have attempted to reproduce the artistry of its engravings. Few early tourists recorded the journey before the Denver and

Rio Grande Railroad was built into Durango or Otto Mears into Silverton. A deserted ranch at Hermosa is mentioned, the occupants had hidden out during an Indian alarm at the neighboring ranch where a fort had been constructed.

History of Colorado published by the State Historical Society and the Natural History Society of Colorado, Linderman Co., Inc., Denver, 1927, contains a treatise on the "Indians" written by Arthur J. Fynn. This is authoritative and should be available at any Colorado library. Colorado histories compiled by Stone and Hall tell much the same story. They all have the same weakness in that the Meeker Massacre of 1879 deals dramatically with events but with a wealth of additional information concerning the Utes and their culture.

The Smithsonian Scientific Series of 1934 includes in Volume Four, "North American Indians" compiled by Rose A. Palmer. The Utes are completely ignored in the text. They are mentioned briefly in a classification of language as being a tribe of Shoshonean stock with the Shoshone, Paiute, Hopi, and Comanche listing the present population of Utes in Utah and Colorado at 2,000.

In an interesting volume, the *Complete History* by Benson J. Lossing, L.L.D., was published for the Home Educational League of America in 1889. It is a thick, pompous volume rich in portrait engravings and presidential bibliographies. Here, again, the Meeker Massacre represents the story of the Utes. This is especially interesting in view of the fact that the annexation of Colorado Territory as a State during the same year is completely ignored.

At the End of the Santa Fe Trail, by Sister Blendina Segale, Ohio Columbian Press, 1932, presents a marvelous picture of early territorial days. Sister Blendina mentions the Utes. She was responsible for saving the life of a Ute Chieftain's son by her skill as a nurse while she was located at Trinidad, Colorado. She earned the Chieftain's gratitude and her school's immunity from Ute raids.

A glance at any tourist map reveals the Ute place names, Ute Park, Ute Creek, Ute Peak, that remain as Monuments with us. The Spanish Peaks were claimed by the Utes. Chipeta had marked the Old Ute Trail from Colorado Springs westward into South Park. Cimarron, Saguache and Gunnison are all sites of Ute campsites. To the south of the Cimarron River near Taos and the Spanish Peaks in Southeastern Colorado mark the home range of the Utes and were accidentally allied with Jicarilla Apaches. Early residents of Taos and Cimarron regarded the Utes and Apaches in the same light. Kit Carson dominates the lives in the early trading post at Taos, where, in 1854, he was appointed Indian Agent for "The Utahs and Apaches." The Denver Art Museum Series of Indian leaflets published an article on "Ute Indians, No. 10," which costs ten cents and presents an authentic outline of what we know about the Ute Indians. They also publish "Material Culture Notes." This matter brings up the difficulty of tracing any Ute habits. They are closely allied to the Apache.

Our so called "Ute Saddle Blanket" donated by Senator George West who recorded, "I won this blanket in a horse race from Red Cloud in 1878. Red Cloud was a sub-chief of the Utes at Ute Mountain. This blanket was credited a Ute work, but I know the Utes did not do any work of this kind and that at this time they thought any work be degrading—they were warriors. I asked Red Cloud who made the blanket and he said the Cheyennes. He depicted how he killed the Cheyenne Chief and acquired the blanket and many ponies."

Lillian White Spencer is a Coloradoan and a poet of note. She is the daughter of a former editor of the *Denver Post* who is remembered for his famous editorials signed "F.W.W." Lillian White Spencer is a poet of increasing power. Her Ute Indian poem, "The Bear Dance," was published in *Frontier* of March 1932. This is a poem describing the Ute Indian Bear Dance, a pictorial dramatic presentation of the philosophy of waking the bear from winter hibernation and leading up to a spring mating of the Utes. Other Indian poems of hers have been published by the *New Mexico Magazine*. She took an active part in the statewide agitation to establish a prominent monument to the memory of Chief Ouray.

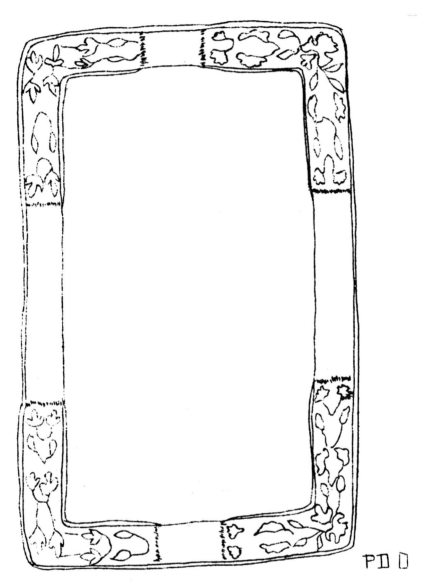

Saddle blanket is 44" long, 31 1/2" wide. 4" wide border made of red trade blanket with beaded floral design, has been repaired with section of blue trade blanket.

Another poem devoted to a Ute Indian theme is by Eugene Field, written when he was a Denver journalist and as Chipeta brought the Meeker Massacre news to the camp of Ouray, her husband and the only Ute with the authority to put a stop to the cruel treatment of the Meeker Massacre captives.

We have been unable to find Ernest Whitney's poem mentioned in *Ute Legends*.

A vivid account of the Meeker Massacre is given by Paul L. Wellman, in his *Death on the Prairie*, published by the Macmillan Company in 1936. An account of the subsequent imprisonment of Utes who took part in the Massacre and the final Massacre of the "stir-crazy" prisoners by the Utes who judged them incapable of carrying on their old habits is sympathetically treated in this book.

Our most fertile source of information is like the "lost" mines of the Spaniards. Although "lost" it is probably not yet destroyed. Miss Sadie Sullivan's father, Mr. Barry Sullivan, was adopted into the Ute tribe and for many years kept note of material that described his experiences and the information gleaned at first hand. His stenographer knew of the book but after his death in an auto accident, his law library was sold and the notebook was never located by his daughter, although everyone concerned knew she wanted to keep that record.

Mr. Sullivan had defended Utes in several cases, and one client had his squaw make a Ute doll to give to his small daughter, Sadie. A detailed description of its construction is included in this series, loaned to us by Miss Sadie Sullivan for that purpose. Mr. Sullivan had kept notes on his experiences during his "initiation" into the tribe, once had allowed the Ute Medicine Man to conduct a "sing" for him when he was ill. Mr. Sullivan, a Harvard Law School graduate, had established his guardianship with the Utes so that nothing was attempted by them until they had consulted his advise. He was influential in persuading rioters during Meeker Massacre to cease. It was a common sight to see Utes squatting about his porch or office hallway awaiting the solution of their difficulties.

It is doubtful if general knowledge of religious ceremony exists among the Utes themselves. For many years the native Sun Dance and Bear Dance were suppressed and little is known of their significance

As the final work on this pamphlet was undertaken, Marvin K. Opler, with his wife and infant son, came to see the Ute collection at The Durango Public Library. He had made a field study of the Southern Utes in 1936-1937. His interpreter was Chief Antonio Buck. He had many opportunities for first hand observations of Ute Culture. His published thesis on his investigations appeared in *Acculturation in Seven American Indian Tribes* edited by Ralph D. Linton, Appleton-Century, New York, 1940, pp. 119-203. Also in *Southwestern Lore*, September 1941. Mr. Opler feels that he had identified Ute pottery, but we have no record which indicates that the Utes either made or used pottery.

Mr. Barry Sullivan had forty-nine chief-patterned blankets, all gifts of Utes, but made by Navajos. It is quite likely that they had traded with the Pueblos also. Each Pueblo specializes in a certain color and design. Mr. Opler has a type of red pottery he believes to be typical of the Utes. We confess our inability to produce any key to the problem of separating Ute crafts such as their beading from that of the Sioux, or their basketry from that of the Apache. Ute bead work may be tested by a rule of threes. That is, you count a design repeated three times or in sets of threes. Mr. Opler and I merrily counted out the beaded designs of those known to be Ute, and found that it held true with many varieties of beading. We have known for a long time that the rule of four is constantly carried out in Navajo culture. We will watch for the rule of three in order to report to Mr. Opler that his scheme is consistently verified.

UTE BURIAL

By Helen Sloan Daniels

UTE BURIAL

By Helen Sloan Daniels

In a communication received from Dr. A.J. McDonald, physician to the Los Pinos Indian Agency, Colorado, a description is given of crevice or rock-fissure burial which follows: (B.A.E. No. 1, 1880, pg. 27.)

"As soon as death takes place the event is at once announced by the medicine man, and without loss of time the squaws are busily engaged in preparing the corpse for the grave. This does not take long; whatever articles of clothing may have been on the body at the time of death are not removed. The dead man's limbs are straightened out, his weapons of war laid by his side and his robes and blankets wrapped securely and snugly around him, and now everything is ready for the burial. It is the custom to secure, if possible, for the purpose of wrapping up the corpse, the robes and blankets in which the Indian died. At the same time that the body is being fitted for interment, the squaws have immediate care of it, together with all the other squaws in the neighborhood keep up a continued chant or dirge, the dismal evidence of which may, when the congregation of women is large, be heard for quite a long distance. The death song is not a mere inarticulate howl of distress; it embraces expressions eulogistic in character, but whether or not any particular formula of words is adopted on such occasion is a question which I am unable, with the materials at my disposal, to determine with any degree of certainty.

The next duty falling to the lot of the squaws is that of placing the dead man on a horse and conducting the remains to the spot chosen for burial. This is in the cleft of a rock, and, so far as can be ascertained, it has always been customary among the Utes to select sepulchers of this character. From descriptions given by Mr. Harris, who has several times been fortunate enough to discover remains, it would appear that no superstitious ideas are held by this tribe with respect to the position in which the body is placed, the space accommodation of the sepulcher probably regulating the matters; and from the same source I learn that is not usual to find the remains of more than one Indian deposited in one grave. After the body has been received into the cleft, it is well covered with pieces of rock to protect it against the ravages of wild animals. The chant ceases, the squaws disperse, and the burial ceremonies are at an end. The men during all this time have not been idle, though they have in no way participated in the preparation of the body, have not joined the squaws in chanting their praises to the memory of the dead, and have not even as mere spectators attended the funeral, yet they have had their duties to perform. In conformity with a long-established custom, all the personal belongings of the deceased are immediately destroyed. His horses and his cattle are shot, and his wigwam furniture burned. The performance of this part of the ceremonies is assigned to the men; a duty quite in accord with their taste and inclinations. Occasionally the destruction of horses and other property is of considerable magnitude, but usually this is not the case, owing to a practice existing with them of distributing their property among their children when they are of a very tender ago, retaining to themselves only what is necessary to meet everyday requirements.

The widow "goes into mourning" by smearing her face with a substance composed of pitch and charcoal. The application is made but once, and is allowed to remain on until it wears off. This is the only mourning of which I have any knowledge.

The ceremonies observed on the death of a female are the same as those in the case of a male, except that no destruction of property takes place in burial of women and of course no weapons are deposited with the corpse. Should a youth die while under the superintendence of white men, the Indians will not as a rule have anything to do with the interment of the body. In a case of the kind which occurred at this agency some time ago, the squaws prepared the body in the usual manner; the men of the tribe selected a spot for burial, and the employees at the agency, after digging a grave and depositing the corpse therein, filled it up according to the fashion of civilized people, and then at the request of the Indians rolled large fragments of rock on top. Great anxiety was exhibited by the Indians to have the employees perform the service as expeditiously as possible.

Within the past year Ouray, the Ute chief living at the Los Pinos Agency, died and was buried, so far as could be ascertained, in a rock fissure or cave seven or eight miles from the agency.

(A current belief of the Utes is that the lost son of Ouray will return and be the Messiah who will lead the present tribes as Ouray once did. An account of the kidnapping is in "Efforts to Recover the Stolen Son of Chief Ouray" by Ann Woodbury Hafen in the *Colorado Magazine*, Number 2, March 1939.)

Mrs. Mary Anne Frost died in the spring of 1928. She was about forty-five years of age and was a member of the Buckskin family. Neighborly gifts of soups, etc., were given during her illness. During this time medicine men from various parts of the country succeeded each other in attendance, but failed to bring about a cure.

Mrs. E. R. Jacques witnessed the procedure of the funeral preparations. After Mrs. Frost died various personal belongings were placed about her, such as buckskin, beads, and needles wrapped in a bundle placed at the foot of the coffin. Hers is a wealthy family and numerous friends and relatives encircled the coffin and paused by her head to strip from their own presence bracelets, necklaces and rings which were placed upon her body.

High shrill cries and wails began with the realization of her death and continued until the time of her burial which occurred the same day. The funeral procession in care of the Agency proceeded to the town where she was buried in the Ignacio cemetery.

At dusk the husband returned to the ranch home with his only child, a ten year old son. Bedding and personal belongings of his wife were loaded into a wagon. No one knows whether he took them out and burned them or buried them.

BIBLIOGRAPHY

BIBLIOGRAPHY

These references are in The Durango Public Library.

CATLIN, George, *Boys Life*, My Life Among the Indians. Edited and Biographical Sketch by Mary Gay Humpreys, Illus., New York, Scribners, 1911.

DOUGLAS, Frederick H., Denver Art Museum, Indian leaflet series 1930-date: No. 10 *Ute Indians*, No. 16 *Apache Indians*, No. 19 *Plains Indians Tipi*, No. 29 *Indians Musical and Noise Making Instruments*.

ESCALANTE, Fray Silvestre Velez De, *Diary and Travels*: translated by Harris, W.R. "Catholic Church in Utah." Intermountain Catholic Press, 1909.

FERRIS, W.A., *Life in the Rocky Mountains*, "The Utes and their Country." (May 1834) Page 262. Old West Publishing Co. 1940.

FREMONT, J.G., *Report of the Exploring Expedition to the Rocky Mountains and to Oregon and California*, Blair and Rives, 1845.

FYNN, Arthur J., "Indians," *History of Colorado*, State Historical Society and Natural History Society of Colorado. Linderman Co. Inc., Denver, 1927.

GARRARD, Lewis H., *Wah-To-Yah, The Taos Trail* (1845) Arthur H. Clark Southern Historical Series 1938.

GRINNELL, George Bird, *Two Great Scouts and their Pawnes Battalion*, The Arthur H. Clark Co., 1928. "Indians of To-day," Duffield & Co., 1911. "The Story of the Indians," D. Appleton and Company, 1906.

HALL, Frank , *History of the State of Colorado*, Vol. I-IV, Blakely Printing Co., 1889.

HAYDEN, F.V., *Tenth Annual Report of the U.S. Geological and Geological Survey of the Territories, embracing Colorado and Parts of Adjacent Territories (1876)* Government Printing Office, 1878.

HODGE, Frederick Webb, *Handbook of American Indians*, Part II, page 847 (Photo) Government Printing Office, 1912.

HOLLING, Holling C., *The Book of Indians*, Illus., Platt and Munk, 1935.

HRDLICKA, Ales, "Physiological and Medical Observations," Government Printing Office, Bulletin 34, 1908.

JAMES, George Wharton, "Indian Basketry and How to Make Baskets," Pasadena, 1903.

LOSSING, Benson J., *Complete History*, Home Educational League of America, 1889.

MOOREHEAD, Warren K., *The American Indians*, Andover Press, 1914.

PLEER, Rose A., *North American Indians*, Smithsonian Scientific Series of 1934.

POWELL,J.W., B.A.E. Report 1878, Burials B.A.E. Report 1878. Letter from Dr. A.J. McDonald, Los Pinos Agency, 1889.

WISSLER, Clark, *Indians of the United States*, 1940.

COLORADO (AMERICAN GUIDE SERIES)
INDEX 1941, SONS OF COLORADO

AYRES, Mary C., "The Founding of Durango," Colorado, May 1930.

AYRES, Mary C., "History of Fort Lewis, Colorado," May, 1931.

CHACON, Major, "(Memoirs) Campaign Against Utes and Apaches in Southern Colorado, 1855," May, 1934.

CLARKE, A.K., "The Utes Visit My Ranch on the Plains," August, 1928.

DAWSON, T.F., Major Thomson, "Chief Ouray and the Utes," May 1930 (Photo).

DURKEY, Elmer R., "The Thornburgh Battle with the Utes on Milk Creek," May, 1936.

HAFEN, Ann Woodburg, "Stolen Son of Chief Ouray," *Colorado Magazine*, March, 1939.

HAFEN, LeRoy R., Editorial Notes, "Chipeta," July 1935.

HAFEN, LeRoy R., "The Fort Pueblo Massacre and the Punitive Expedition against the Utes," March, 1927.

FINE, Eben G., "The Ute and the Boulder Semi-Centennial Celebration," March 1939.

JACKSON, W.H., "First Official Visit to the Cliff Dwellings, May 1924." Photographing the Colorado Rockies Fifty Years Ago For the United States Geological Surveys, March, 1926. "A Visit to the Los Pinos Agency in 1874," (Diary) November, 1938.

LONDONER, Wolfe, "Colorow, Renegade Chief, Dines Out," May, 1931.

McGUE, D.R., "John Taylor, Slave-Born Colorado Pioneer," September, 1941.

NANKIVELL, John H. Major, "Colorado's Last Indian 'War.'" November, 1933.

RICE, Jay, Elial, "Pioneering in Southern Colorado," May, 1937.

RICHIE, Eleanor, "General Mano Mocha of the Utes and Spanish Policy in Indian Relations," July, 1935.

ROBINSON, Anna Florence, As Told By Fred Taylor, "Pioneering in Southwestern Colorado," July 1935.

RUSSELL, James, "Conditions and Customs of Present-Day Ute in Colorado," May, 1929.

SANFORD, A. B., "Reminiscences of Kit Carson, Jr." An interview and Notes, July, 1929.

STOBIE, Charles, S., "With the Indians in Colorado," March, 1930.

WHITE, Laurie C. Manson, "Pagosa Springs, Colorado," May, 1932.

WIEGEL, Mrs. C.W., "The Re-burial of Chief Ouray," (Photo) October, 1928 "The Death of Ouray, Chief of the Utes," (Photo) September 1930.

WHITTIER, Florence E., "Grave of Chief Ouray," (Photography by Wm. L. Tisdel, Denver, Colorado) November, 1924.

ZINGG, R.M., "The Ute Indians in Historical Relation to Proto-Azteco-Tanoan Culture," July, 1938.

SOUTHWESTERN LORE

CASEY, Pearle R., "Two Tales of the Utes," Vol. IV, No. 1, June, 1937. Buckskin Charley, Chief of the Utes, Vol. IV, No. 2.

HURST, C. T., "A Ute Shelter in Saguache County, Colorado" Museum of Archaeology, Gunnison, December, 1939.

OPLER, M. K., "A Colorado Ute Indian Bear Dance," September, 1941.

WEYRAUCH, Genevieve, Ouray, Chief of the Utes," March 1939, Vol. IV, No. 4.

MISCELLANEOUS MAGAZINE ARTICLES

"Besieged by the Utes (Meeker)" *Century*, Vol. 42, page 837.

Sun Dance Outlook, Vol. 97, page 65.

"Wrongs of the Ute Indians," Vol. 8 *Forum*.

Costume, color plate XI, page 611, *National Geographic Magazine*, May, 1936.

Castle, Mrs. Newton, "Yes I Knew Chipeta," *Sunset Slope*, May, 1940.

NEW MEXICO

BARRETT, S. M., *Geronimo's Story of his Life*, Duffield Co., 1906.

DRANNAN, Captain Wm. F., *Thirty-one Years on the Plains and the Mountains*, Rhodes and McClure Publishing Co., 1900.

SABIN, E.L., *Kit Carson Days*, Chicago, 1914.

SEGALE, Sister Blendina, *At the End of the Santa Fe Trail*, Ohio Columbian Press, 1932.

COLORADO UTES

BYRNE, Barnard J., *A Frontier Life of an Army Surgeon* (Fort Lewis, 1881).

CHAPIN, F. H., *The Land of the Cliff Dwellers*, W.B. Clark and Company, 1892.

DARLEY, G. M., *Pioneering in the San Juan*, Fleming H. Revell Company, 1899.

FREMONT, J.C., *Report of the Exploring Expedition to the Rocky Mountains and to Oregon and California*, Blair and Rives, 1845.

GILLMORE, Frances, Wetherill, Louise Wedo, *Traders to the Navajoes*, Joe Houghton-Mifflin, 1934.

HOWBERT, Irving, *Indians of the Pikes Peak Region*, The Knickerbocker Press, 1914.

INGERSOLL, Ernest, *The Crest of the Continent*, R.R. Donelly and Sons Co., Chicago, 1890.

JOCKNICK, Sidney, *Early Days on the Western Slope of Colorado*, Carson Harper Co., 1913.

MONROE, Arthur W., *San Juan Silver*, 1940.

OPLER, M.K., "Acculturation in Seven American Tribes," edited by Ralph Linton, D. Appleton, *Century*, N.Y., 1940.

WELLMAN, Paul I., *Death on the Prairie*, Macmillan Co., 1933, (Apache) Death on the Desert, 1935.

MANUSCRIPTS

FRICK, Ford, "Ute Legends," *National Republican*.

McCALL, Albert M., "Outline of Ute Culture."

McCARTEY, Nell B., "Indians of the San Juan Basin."

McCLOUD, WILSON, RITTER, "Southern Ute Indians."

MUSSER, Lo Visa, "Reminiscences of the San Juan Basin."

WARRSON, D. H., "Statement to Mr. Morris Cleavinger," February 8, 1936.

WEST, Senator George, Letter.

MAPS

FISCHER, Emil B., "Author of the Mining Map of Red Mountain, the mining region of the San Juan, Ouray, San Miguel and Dolores Counties, Southwestern Colorado, 1891."

FOREST SERVICE MAPS of San Juan National Forest. Uintah Reservation, Utah, National Geographic Magazine, May 31, 1936.

PHOTOGRAPHS
ETCHINGS, Dixon, Dr. Joseph, "The Vanishing Race," Doubleday, Page & Company, 1913.
GARLAND, Hamlin, "The Book of the American Indian," Pictures by Frederick Remington, Harper & Brothers, 1923.
SEYMOUR, Flora W., "The Story of the Red Man," Longmans Green and Co., 1929.

SMITHSONIAN REPORTS
MASON, Otis T., "Aboriginal skin-dressing," A study based on material in the United States National Museum (with Plates LXI-XCIII).
MASON, Otis T., "Basket-work of the North American Aborigines," 1884.
MASON, Otis T., "Aboriginal American Basketry: Studies in a Textile Art without Machinery," 1902.
MASON, Otis T., "North American Bow, Arrows and Quivers," 1893.
MASON, Otis T., "Primitive Travel and Transportation," Curator, Department of Ethnology, U. S. National Museum, 1894.
MASON, Otis T., "Throwing-Sticks in the National Museum," Smithsonian Report, Washington D.C. 1884.
MASON, Otis T., "Traps of the American Indians, a study in Psychology and Invention," 1901.

POEMS
FIELDS, Eugene, "To Chipeta."
SPENCER, Lillian White, "Bear Dance," Frontier, March, 1932.

INTRODUCTION TO AMERICAN INDIAN ART
The Exposition of Indian Tribal Arts 1931

John Sloan
Oliver La Forge
Herbert J. Spinden
Mary Austin
Alice Corbin Henderson
Laura Adams Armer
Ruth Gaines

Kenneth M. Chapman
Neil M. Judd
Charles C. Willoughby
E. W. Gifford
Mary Lois Kissell
Williams C. Orchard

CLIPPINGS
"Ute Agency News," *Durango News* weekly column.

Printed in the United States
144050LV00002B/11/P

9 781932 738605